THE
SHROPSHIRE
CAKES AND ALE TRAIL

Bob Bibby

First published in Great Britain by Pierrepoint Press 2007.

A CIP record for this book is available from the British Library.

ISBN   978 0 9533196 4 0

Cover design by Clare Brayshaw

Typeset, printed and bound in Great Britain by:
York Publishing Services Ltd
64 Hallfield Road
Layerthorpe
York
YO31 7ZQ
Tel: 01904 431213   Website: www.yps-publishing.co.uk

THE
SHROPSHIRE
CAKES AND ALE TRAIL

Bob Bibby

With illustrations by Wendy Poulton

Published by Pierrepoint Press

Other books by Bob Bibby

Travel Writing

Grey Paes and Bacon: From the Heart of the Black Country

Dancing with Sabrina: The River Severn –
a Journey from Source to Sea

Special Offa: A Walk along Offa's Dyke

On the Wall with Hadrian

(Published by Eye Books)

Crime Fiction

Be a Falling Leaf

Bird on the Wing

The Liquidator

The Llareggub Experience

(Published by Pierrepoint Press)

Dedication

To the memory of my mother, Christina Bibby.

Acknowledgements

I would like to thank Susan Sharp of the *Shropshire Ramblers Association*, Alan Garner of *Secret Hills Walking Holidays* and Paul Francis, who gave invaluable advice about parts of the route. Steve Clarke accompanied me on much of the route and pointed out misleading directions, for which I am most grateful.

Thanks too are due to Sue Yardley of *Bridgnorth Visitor Information Centre*, Tim King of *South Shropshire Tourism*, Helen and Geoff Lewis, Angel Scott and Ash James, who read parts or all of earlier versions of this book and provided helpful comments.

Thanks also to Wendy Poulton for her splendid illustrations and to Nick Davis of *Hobsons Brewery* for his kindness in sponsoring the challenge element of this walk and for his support in the book's development. Finally I would like to thank my wife Enid who sparked the original idea and who continues to inspire me.

"Dost thou think, because thou art virtuous, there shall be no more cakes and ale?"

Sir Toby Belch in *Twelfth Night*

CONTENTS

INTRODUCTION

Origins of the Trail

Shropshire has long been one of my favourite walking counties. The first long-distance walk I ever did was the Six Shropshire Summits hike and I have walked throughout the shire over the years, particularly in its southern part. For some years I had harboured the notion of creating my own long-distance walk around Shropshire and it was while visiting some of the picturesque market towns in the south of Shropshire that I hit upon the idea of *The Shropshire Cakes and Ale Trail*. The idea was to build a seven-day circular walk, averaging about fifteen miles a day, linking up those towns and ensuring a good pub for lunchtime ale, a good café for afternoon cakes and a choice of pubs for evening ales.

At that stage I was thinking of the reputation that Shropshire has carved out for itself in recent years as being a gourmet's paradise with its award-winning restaurants, its outstanding Real Ale breweries and its astonishing range of suppliers of locally-produced food.

At the same time, however, I had been been reading much literature from the Civil War period as part of my research for a crime novel I was planning to write and, while reading about the misery of those times, was constantly reminded of Sir Toby Belch's anguished protest at the restrictions which Malvolio, that arch Puritan, was seeking to impose on Toby and his merry friends:

> *"Dost thou think, because thou art virtuous, there shall be no more cakes and ale?"*

Sir Toby's cry echoes down the centuries against all those who would restrict the pleasures of life, who want us to drink only water and eat only salads, and whose idea of exercise is walking on a treadmill in a gym with a heart monitor attached to you.

So I set about creating *The Shropshire Cakes and Ale Trail*, partly in response to the doom and gloom so prevalent in much of our current polity and partly to provide a real opportunity for those who enjoy walking to step it out over the Shropshire hills and dales and at the same time to enjoy some of those gourmet delights mentioned earlier, in particular the Real Ales in some of Shropshire's great pubs. This walk, though challenging in distance, is great fun too, so enjoy it and say, *"Yah boo sucks,"* to all the naysayers of the world.

Shropshire, like most counties nowadays, is criss-crossed by a number of other long-distance paths, some of whose routes in places coincide with mine and each of which has its own attractions. Predominant is *The Shropshire Way*, a long circular path running through the whole county from Shrewsbury to Ludlow in southern Shrophire, through Ironbridge in the east then Wem in the north, before returning to the county town. *The Jack Mytton Way* is a 100-mile bridlepath starting and finishing in Cleobury Mortimer mostly in the southern part of the county. *The Offa's Dyke Path* skirts Shropshire's western wing and the *Severn Way* follows Britain's longest river as it weaves its way from the Welsh border into Worcestershire. Many of these paths I have walked but none fulfilled all that I wanted, particularly in terms of offering good accommodation, good pubs and good cafés. That is why I have created my own route. Shropshire is a largely agricultural county, so virtually all of *The Shropshire Cakes and Ale Trail* is through countryside, following public rights of way or, occasionally, minor roads.

Nikolaus Pevsner in his masterly book *Buildings of England: Shropshire* states that the greatest attraction of the county is that *"it does not attract too many"*. That is as true today as it was when his book was first published fifty years ago. Hardy walkers still tend to head for the Peak District, the Lake District or Scotland for their adventures and, although none of the scenery may be as spectacular as that to be found in those areas, nonetheless Shropshire has its own special attractions. Not least are its hills – the Long Mynd, Stiperstones, Wenlock Edge, Caer Caradoc, and the Clees. All of these provide magnificent walking opportunities and terrific views from their tops. It was no accident that the Shropshire Hills was one of the first areas to be designated, in 1958, as an Area of Outstanding Natural Beauty. It stretches from the Wrekin to the Clun Forest and from Stiperstones to the Clee Hills and you will visit much of it on *The Shropshire Cakes and Ale Trail*.

Just as fascinating are the market towns which I have used as the base points for each section of *The Shropshire Cakes and Ale Trail*. Bridgnorth, Cleobury Mortimer, Ludlow, Clun, Bishop's Castle, Church Stretton and Much Wenlock all have their own intriguing histories and secrets, as well as providing plenty of opportunities for walkers to take rest in a range of accommodation, take cake in the cafés and take ale in the characterful pubs and hotels. The route also leads walkers through or past many other places of interest – Norman churches, stately homes, archaeological sites, historical ruins, fallen castles, Iron Age hillforts, and other more modern curiosities – as well as introducing them to some of the colourful characters who have contributed to the spirit of the county.

Although I have begun and ended my route in Bridgnorth, walkers may wish to find their own point of entry. Likewise, although the route is described in seven sections, each of which is approximately 15 miles long, walkers who do not have the opportunity to follow the route for seven consecutive days, or who do not have the energy to cover these distances, will find their own ways of managing. My hope is that any who follow in my footsteps will experience as much pleasure as I did in walking *The Shropshire Cakes and Ale Trail*.

The Round House, Aston-on-Clun

Planning the Walk

Those used to long days of walking on a regular basis should have no problems in covering *The Shropshire Cakes and Ale Trail*. A reasonable amount of stamina and fitness should sustain such walkers on the journey (as will the cakes and ale!). Be aware, however, that there is a difference between a good Sunday walk and walking fifteen miles every day for a week. Getting good miles under your feet in preparation will pay off in terms of your enjoyment and comfort during your journey.

As regards equipment and clothing, I prefer to travel as light as possible but it is essential to have a good waterproof jacket and trousers. Boots (well worn in, of course) are necessary too, since the terrain in places can be quite demanding and ankles need support. If journeying in hot weather, you may be tempted to wear shorts but be prepared that at such times and in some places paths can become overgrown with nettles and/or brambles, so keep your overtrousers handy. A walking pole is a useful accessory for warding off such vegetation, as well as for shooing away inquisitive cows. Be aware also that some parts of the trail, especially where it coincides with a bridleway, can be very muddy. If arranging accommodation in advance, you might consider posting changes of clothing, new maps etc to and from where you are staying.

The walk can be done at any time of the year, though potential walkers need to beware of the River Severn flooding as you leave Bridgnorth and, as the story of the Reverend Carr at Church Stretton shows, snow on the Long Mynd and on the other high points can make walking treacherous and indeed dangerous. The best period is between May and October when you are likely to enjoy the attractions of the countryside at its brightest and when temperatures should be at their most accommodating.

Ordnance Survey Maps

The following Ordnance Survey 1:25000 maps are essential for following the route. Each has been referenced in the appropriate section.

Explorer 201: Knighton & Presteigne
Explorer 203: Ludlow
Explorer 216: Welshpool & Montgomery
Explorer 217: The Long Mynd & Wenlock Edge
Explorer 218: Wyre Forest & Kidderminster
Explorer 242: Telford, Ironbridge & The Wrekin

Explanatory Notes

The Shropshire Cakes and Ale Trail guide to the walk itself is set out in seven sections, each with its own introduction which includes a gradient summary, a brief description of the terrain for that section and a mileage chart. Each section is then further subdivided into subsections of varying distances which have a narrative and diagrams of the route on one page, with illustrations and text about features encountered during the walk on the opposite page. The diagrams are NOT to scale but are intended to indicate the direction of the trail, particularly at junctions of paths and/or roads. The diagrams should be used in combination with the relevant Ordnance Survey Explorer Map.

Each section concludes with photographs of the town where that day's walking finishes, together with a brief history of the place and an account of some of the celebrities whose names linger there. Finally, and this book would be pointless without it, there is a guide to some of the cafés and pubs in that town, together with an accommodation list and other essential information about facilities (Post Office, bank ATMs, Visitor Information Centre, Transport connections) in each. Naturally, other walkers may find different cafés and different pubs to the ones I have indicated. The selection is entirely my own and therefore entirely idiosyncratic. The accommodation list is not a recommended list but merely an indication of possibilities. Be aware, of course, that changes do occur and these listings will not be accurate for ever.

N.B. If planning walks on Saturdays and Sundays, it is worth checking out the Shropshire Hills Shuttle buses which operate in all of the scenic parts of the route between April and October. Details and timetables from any of the Visitor Information Centres.

The Shropshire Cakes and Ale Challenge

Finally, if you are the sort of walker who likes to have evidence that you have completed the challenge of *The Shropshire Cakes and Ale Trail*, there are 7 stamping points en route for you to collect a stamp in the appropriate space inside the back cover of this guidebook. They are as follows:

Section 1: The Fighting Cocks, Stottesdon
Section 2: The Kremlin, Clee Hill
Section 3: The Kangaroo Inn, Aston-on-Clun
Section 4: The Crown, Newcastle-on-Clun

Section 5: The Horsehoe Inn, Bridges
Section 6: The Wenlock Edge Inn, Wenlock Edge
Section 7: The Acton Arms, Morville

N.B. If you find that the pub is closed on your arrival, alternative stamping places are indicated.

Any walker who presents their book with seven stamps in the appropriate spaces at the end of their walk at any of the following places:

The King's Arms, Cleobury Mortimer
The Church Inn, Ludlow,
The White Horse Inn, Clun
The Castle Hotel, Bishop's Castle
The Buck's Head, Church Stretton
The George and Dragon, Much Wenlock
The Railwayman's Arms, Bridgnorth

will be rewarded with a free pint of Hobsons beer (N.B. only one pint per book).

I am most eternally grateful to Nick Davis of *Hobsons Brewery* in Cleobury Mortimer for sponsoring this element of the walk.

Countryside Code

- Be safe – plan ahead and follow any signs
- Leave gates and property as you find them
- Protect plants and animals, and take your litter home
- Keep dogs under close control
- Consider other people

ADVICE TO READERS

You are advised that, although every effort has been made to ensure the accuracy of this guidebook, changes may occur. It is sensible to check in advance on transport and accommodation but rights of way can also sometimes be amended.

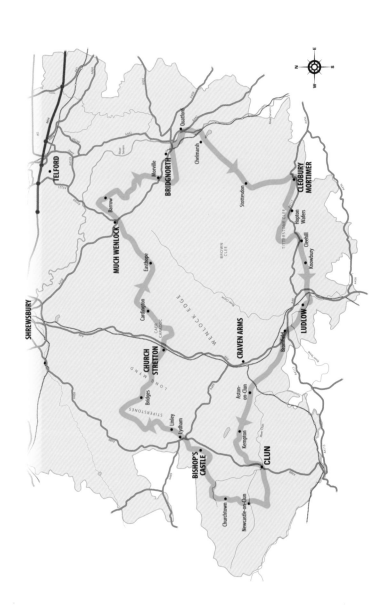

BRIDGNORTH – CLEOBURY MORTIMER

OS Map: Explorer 218

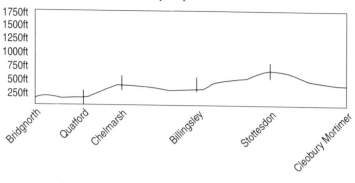

This is a relatively easy day's walking, beginning with a leisurely stroll out of Bridgnorth along the attractive banks of the River Severn, once the major trading thoroughfare in England. At the end of the 17th century it was the busiest river in Europe after the Meuse, its waters filled with flat-bottomed boats with square sails, known as Severn trows, plus coracles for fishing and punts to ferry folk from one bank to the other.

After passing Quatford, the route takes you inland past Chelmarsh and across country to Billingsley where The Cape of Good Hope is the best chance of a weekday lunch pint. A little-walked route then leads you to the unspoilt village of Lower Chorley and through a delightful bridlepath to Stottesdon. Both of these villages have pubs, The Duck and The Fighting Cocks respectively, open at weekends.

Finally you follow in the steps of the postman-poet on the Simon Evans Way into the ancient town of Cleobury Mortimer, with its crooked spire, its Georgian houses and its fine selection of opportunities for cakes and ale.

PLACE	DAILY MILES	TOTAL MILES
Bridgnorth	–	
Quatford	2	2
Chelmarsh	5	5
Billingsley	7.5	7.5
Stottesdon	10.5	10.5
Cleobury Mortimer	15	15

BRIDGNORTH – CLEOBURY MORTIMER
(15 miles)

Bridgnorth to Chelmarsh *(5 miles)*

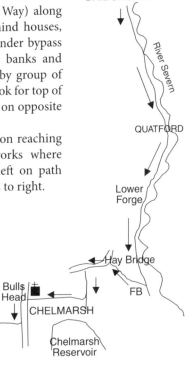

- From paved area by bridge over River Severn, take footpath (Severn Way) along Hightown bank of Severn behind houses, through waterside fields and under bypass road, then through tree-lined banks and more waterside meadows till, by group of houses on other side of river, look for top of Quatford Church ahead of you on opposite bank.
- About one mile further on, upon reaching Lower Forge, once an ironworks where nailmaking took place, keep left on path close to river, ignoring all paths to right.
- By sign for *"Albrighton Anglers,"* just before an ornate footbridge over Mor Brook, go right on path, through small car park for day-time anglers and night-time lovers, up to junction with B4555 at Hay Bridge.
- Go left on road under bridge (be careful – busy road) and uphill 400 yards to bridleway to left, signposted Dinney Farm.
- Follow bridleway till junction signposted Dinney Farm and go right (Cycle Path 45). Go straight on at Dinney Farm on Cycle Path 45, now also Jack Mytton Way, past edge of Chelmarsh Reservoir (watch out for boats, bikes and birds).
- Where Cycle Path 45 goes right, keep straight ahead on bridleway till junction with B4555, where cross road and turn left passing by Hall Farm with views of Chelmarsh Reservoir behind it till you reach The Bull's Head.

QUATFORD

St Mary's, Quatford

Quatford was where Roger de Montgomery built a church and a castle in 1070. The reason for choosing this site was all to do with a storm at sea, a hollow oak and a hunting trip. Adelisa, wife of the aforesaid Roger, was sailing across the Channel from France to join up with her husband when a fierce storm arose. She vowed to build a church on the spot where she met her husband if she was saved. End of storm, meeting with Roger the Dodger by a hollow oak at Quatford, and hey presto! the building of St Mary's Church, which contains a modern stained glass window of an oak tree in Adelisa's memory.

Roger's son, Robert de Belleme, moved the settlement upstream, to what is now Bridgnorth, some years later, probably because he'd heard of all the pubs there.

CHELMARSH

St Peter's Church was built in 1345 for Hugh de Mortimer. It has a fine Norman doorway. Legend tells of a monk's heart being embedded in its east wall.

Chelmarsh Reservoir, owned by South Staffordshire Water, is a favoured haunt of local birdwatchers, especially in winter. Here you can see swans, geese, ducks and occasional sightings of pintail, goldeneye, goosander and smew. A reed warbler colony now thrives in the specially planted reed-bed along with reed buntings and sedge warblers. Ospreys call in here en route to and from their breeding grounds.

Chelmarsh Reservoir is also the home of Chelmarsh Sailing Club, whose refurbished clubhouse was opened in 2005 by none other than the Princess Royal.

St Peter's, Chelmarsh

Chelmarsh Sailing Club

Chelmarsh to Billingsley (2.5 miles)

- Just before Bull's Head pub in Chelmarsh, turn right down Bakehouse Lane and just past The Glebe take bridleway to left, signposted *"The Loosebox 250 yards"*. Follow this green lane, with distant views of Clee Hills to your right, to reach minor road, where go right.
- Keep on road for approximately half mile till, just after crossing bridge over Borle Brook, go through first gate on left and follow left field boundary to reach wooden gate into woodland.
- Go through gate and take gently rising path through Hook Plantation to metal gate at edge of woodland.
- Go straight ahead across field, aiming for gap in hedge with buildings on horizon and ignoring path to Hook Farm on right.
- At gap in hedge, head diagonally right towards gate adjoining end of treeline coming in from right, aiming for farm buildings.
- Follow line of oak trees through gate and up to further metal gate by large oak tree with farm buildings on right.
- Go over gate and through two fields with stiles between and on to narrow path beside fence to emerge on drive of Cherry Tree House.
- Go right and then right again into Billingsley and Cape of Good Hope.

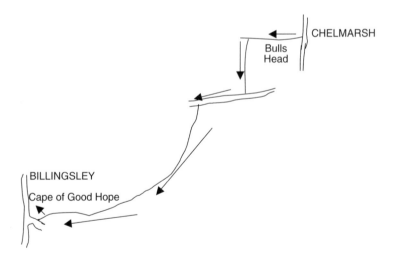

BILLINGSLEY

It's hard to believe that what looks now like a modern dormitory village, with some older properties hidden away from the main road, was once a thriving mining community with a railway that connected its mines to the River Severn.

Billingsley lies at the edge of the Wyre Forest coalfield. The colliery was first developed towards the end of the 18th century by Sir William Pulteney but that early attempt ended in 1822. It was in 1870 that more serious efforts were undertaken to resume mining but there's not a lot of point digging out coal if you can't get it to market, so a railway was begun, which included a two and a half mile inclined plane, to take the coal to Stanley on the River Severn, where it was loaded on to trows and taken down river.

Billingsley colliery closed in 1921 and the railway line closed in 1937. If you look carefully in the surrounding fields, you can see spoil heaps from the mines and the inclined plane is now a footpath.

The Cape of Good Hope

Walton's Polyglot Bible

The Cape of Good Hope is open weekdays from 12.00 to 3.00 pm and all day at weekends. It serves tasty food and has Banks's, Hobsons, and Enville Real Ales. (Tel: 01746-861565).

Thomas Hyde, the biblical scholar, was born in Billingsley in 1636. He was the first Englishman to learn Chinese and contributed to Walton's Polyglot Bible. So now you know!

Billingsley to Stottesdon (3 miles)

- Opposite Cape of Good Hope, take stile in hedge and path across fields to Southall Bank Farm. Cross cattle grid and turn right through gate signed *"Woodlands"* then go left to gate leading to pleasant woodland path.
- Go through small clearing, then downhill on woodland path but turn right before gate at bottom on indistinct path to partially-collapsed footbridge.
- Go diagonally right to stile into field and follow diverted path right along two sides of field to stile, where go straight across two more fields with stile between to stile leading to footpath through Chorley Covert, signposted *"Private Woodlands"*.
- Where path emerges on to road at High Green, go right on road to Lower Chorley and, just before Duck Inn, take bridleway to left.

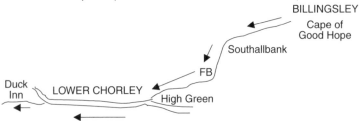

- Take bridleway past telephone box and follow this through lovely woodland way to grounds of Chorley Hall, ignoring footpath to left half way.
- Follow path around Chorley Hall then go left through kissing gate at footpath sign. Follow left side of field down to gate at bottom, where go left on road for 50 yards then, just before bridge, right over waymarked stile in hedge.
- Keep to left of field and look for waymarked stile down to plank over brook and stile, where follow left side of field to further stile. After 50 yards look for stile down left through covert with steps, bridge, and more steps to stile. Here follow right side of field to stile, then another steps/bridge/stile combination. Keep on right side of next field to a further stile/bridge/stile combination.
- Keep to right side of next open field, ignoring waymarked fingerpost up to left, and once past small clump of trees aim for fingerpost straight ahead and subsequent stile diagonally to right.
- Go straight across field, aiming between two large oak trees with church ahead to left, to stile in hedge, where go left on road and immediately right through gate on to bridleway past farm on to road then left into Stottesdon and Fighting Cocks.

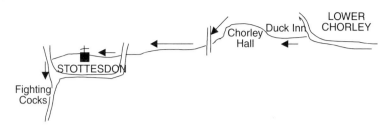

STOTTESDON

The Church of St Mary is one of the most important churches in the whole district, containing an elaborately-carved stone lintel dating to the Anglo-Saxon period, which appears to show a cat or dog and a deer upside down with a net behind them, representing the chase. It also has an ornately-carved Norman font, believed to be the work of the renowned Hereford School of Sculptors, and a 14th century stained glass window.

Norman Font

The Fighting Cocks was the winner at the Deliciously Shropshire Food and Drink Awards in 2005. In 2004, supported by grants from the Countryside Alliance, it opened a shop selling good local produce, including cakes, attached to the pub. Pop in and buy something – it's good for the soul to support local enterprise.

The Fighting Cocks

The Fighting Cocks is an excellent pub, open from 12.00 at weekends only, serving food and Hobsons Real Ales from 12.00 to 2.00 pm. The landlady is prepared to open mid-week for parties by prior arrangement (Tel: 01746-718270).

Stamping point at bar or in shop next door.

Stottesdon to Cleobury Mortimer (4.5 miles)

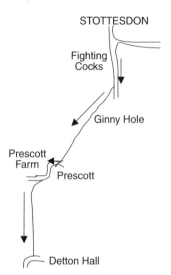

- Take road signposted Cleobury Mortimer past Fighting Cocks out of Stottesdon till you reach footpath on right signposted Simon Evans Way.

- Take this good track down past Ginny Hole and at junction of paths keep straight ahead to stile at end of woodland.

- Go straight ahead to stile in hedge, then through small field, over another stile and, with views of Clee Hills to right and ahead, diagonally left straight across a large field (aim for clump of trees at start of hedge).

- From stile follow path to stile at road junction and Simon Evans Way sign.

- Go right on road past Country Treks sign and, immediately after Prescott Farm, take bridleway/Simon Evans Way to left.

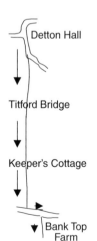

- At three gates, go straight ahead through middle gate on Jack Mytton Way and follow green lane past bench at junction of paths till reaching road, where go right and follow road past Detton Hall Farm.

- Continue on road past Detton Hall till reaching footpath to right before road bends to left.

- Follow this clear footpath to cross River Rea at Titford Bridge, and on past Keeper's Cottage till reaching junction with road.

- Go left and shortly afterwards by Meadowbank bungalow go right to Bank Top Farm.

- Clear track takes you parallel with River Rea past Bank Top Farm, with views of Neen Savage church to your left.

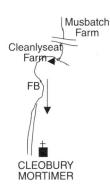

- Continue past Musbatch Farm to minor road.

- Cross road and over stile follow hedge on right of field to stile.

- Over stile go right past Cleanlyseat Farm and follow path round to footbridge and over, then path initially rising to left.

- Follow footpath up past primary school and into Cleobury Mortimer itself by Church of the Virgin Mary.

SIMON EVANS WAY

The Simon Evans Way commemorates the poet-postman of Cleobury Mortimer, Simon Evans. Born in 1895 in Wales, Evans was gassed in the First World War and, on returning to his job as a postman in Liverpool after the war, found the industrial air too difficult and managed to swap with a postie in Cleobury. From 1926 till his death in 1940 Simon Evans completed his rural round on foot from Cleobury Mortimer to Abdon Burf and back. It is estimated he walked some 75,000 miles in that time.

He had a postal hut in Stottesdon, in which he put pen to paper and wrote a total of five books (including one novel) about this South Shropshire area. His writing was stimulated by a correspondence course in English Literature he took from Ruskin College in Oxford, after which he wrote for regional periodicals and gave short talks on BBC radio. It was at the BBC that he met Doris Aldridge, who was "Aunty Doris" on BBC Children's Hour and who, during her time on the show, took the unusual step of using her local Oxfordshire/Gloucestershire dialect when storytelling, which caused a stir in the BBC. Then BBC Director General Sir John Reith stopped her, saying it was not lady-like to speak in dialect. In 1938 Simon married Doris at Bridgnorth Registry Office.

In the late 30's Simon's health deteriorated and he died in a Birmingham hospital in 1940 during one of the many air raids on that city. His ashes were scattered on Abdon Burf. Interest in his life has grown in recent years, thanks to the publication of his biography by Mark Baldwin of the M&M Bookshop in Cleobury Mortimer.

The Simon Evans Way, a 15 mile figure-of-eight route covering much of his postman's round, was inaugurated in 2000 as part of the local Millennium Festival.

CLEOBURY MORTIMER PIX

Talbot Hotel

Pork Pie Shop

Cleobury Well

Hobsons Brewery

Church of Virgin Mary

William Langland Window

CLEOBURY MORTIMER STORY

"A long airy curving street of brick Georgian houses and shops interspersed with genuine half-timber, the Rea brook making a splash at the bottom of the hill. The whole church seems to have slipped out of shape".

John Betjeman

Cleobury (pronounced Clibbury) was a settlement long before the Norman Conquest, as the amusingly-named Castle Toot, site of an Iron Age fort (now a modern house) shows. It took its second name from Ralph de Mortimer, one of William's top brass at the Battle of Hastings. Ralph was sent over to the borders to sort out Edric, the Earl of Shrewsbury (later known as Wild Edric), and he made the castle in Cleobury his main residence.

Successive generations of Mortimers did what most of the Anglo-Norman lords of the time did, that is engage in ding-dongs with their neighbours, marry the neighbours' daughters to resolve those ding-dongs, duff up the Welsh (always a popular occupation) and sometimes get involved in the national scene by fighting for the king of the day. For 400 years the Mortimers were the top dogs in this part of the world, though they moved their headquarters from Cleobury to Ludlow Castle.

Later the wealth of the town grew from the coal, iron and stone being mined on nearby Titterstone Clee, from wood-turning and from paper-making, both of which flourished in the many mills that were driven by the fast-flowing River Rea. For example, Cleobury Mortimer was a major exporter of wooden bowls, dishes and cups in an age when other materials were scarce.

Nowadays, as well as serving the needs of those who work in the town and the surrounding area, its proximity to the West Midlands conurbation makes it an attractive option for those working in the latter. It is also the home of the rather wonderful Hobsons Brewery, which opened in 1992 and whose beers (Best Bitter, Town Crier, Manor Ale, Old Henry, and Mild) you can and MUST sample throughout South Shropshire.

Cleobury Mortimer spreads itself along its High Street, where all its pubs and shops are situated. At the heart of the town is the Church of the Virgin Mary with its crooked spire, the result of its oak beams becoming warped by wind, rain and time. The church is believed to pre-date the arrival of Ralph de Mortimer but the present building is from the 12th century. The church contains a beautiful stained glass window in its nave commemorating William Langland, who is believed to have been born in Cleobury.

CLEOBURY MORTIMER CELEBRITIES

William Langland (1331–1400)

William Langland, allegedly born in Cleobury, was a contemporary of Geoffrey Chaucer and is acknowledged as one of the father figures of English literature. His long poem *The Vision of Piers Plowman*, written in alliterative verse, begins:

> *In a summer season, when soft was the sun,*
> *In rough cloth I robed me, as I a shepherd were,*
> *In a habit like a hermit in his works unholy,*
> *And through the wide world I went, wonders to hear...*

The poem concerns the narrator's quest for the true Christian life, involving a series of dreams about the lives of three allegorical characters, Do-Wel, Do-Bet and Do-Best, (but not Da-Doo-Ron-Ron) who are sought by Piers, the humble plowman of the title.

Billy Penrose (1924–1962)

The jazz pianist Billy Penrose was born in Cleobury and spent his early life there, before making his name with various bands, including those of Ted Heath and Lou Praeger. Penrose is credited with bringing boogie-woogie to Britain and there are recordings of him playing his own boogie-woogie compositions as a 19-year old.

He also toured with Vera Lynn during World War Two, when his favourite party trick was eating razor blades for breakfast and sticking safety pins through his cheeks to entertain the troops. Well, that's jazz!

Simon Evans (1895–1940)

You've already been introduced to Simon Evans, Cleobury's poet-postman, so here's his description of the crooked spire of the Church of the Virgin Mary;

> *Very quaint and very old is this village, but oldest and quaintest of all is the leaning, crooked steeple. It somehow suggests a warped and weather-beaten great-grandparent, silent, watchful, tolerant; perhaps at times, a little annoyed, but more often amused, I think, by the modern things which, of late, move about him.*
> *He appears to have raised one shoulder in a slight shrug and twisted his head a little to enable him to see as much as possible of the High Street while still keeping a watchful eye on the market place.*

CLEOBURY MORTIMER CAKES

POPPY'S TEA ROOMS, Lower Street
Part of the Hammond Hotel complex, offering a wide range of snacks, meals and cakes.

COURTNEY'S TOP NOSH DELI, High Street
A fascinating delicatessen selling great cheeses, meats, pickles and jams and with a café area serving delicious home-made cakes and pies.

CLEOBURY MORTIMER ALE

TALBOT HOTEL, High Street
Serves Hobsons beers. Friendly service. Food served. Nice stone fireplaces. Bar and eating area. Pool table. Hops along the main beam in the bar. Also offers accommodation.

STABLES TAVERN, High Street
Situated down the alleyway next to the Talbot Hotel. Serves Enville Ale and Banks's. Food served. Big black fireplace with lots of trophies. Lots of beams.

KING'S ARMS, High Street
Lovely old-fashioned pub, serving Hobsons and Adnams beers. Background music. Pool room, which can be noisy. Hops along the beams. Food served. Morning coffee and home-made scones also served. Situated opposite Talbot Hotel.

ROYAL FOUNTAIN, High Street
Comfortable pub with sofas and soft chairs, serving Batemans and Abbot Ales. Food served.

BELL INN, High Street
Free house serving Banks's beers. Also the home of the brilliant Bell Inn Brass Band, who rehearse here. Take your ear plugs.

OLD LION INN, High Street
Serves Hobsons beers. A real fire and lots of pine. Pool table. Juke box can be noisy.

CLEOBURY MORTIMER ACCOMMODATION

OLD CIDER HOUSE, 1 Lion Lane, Cleobury Mortimer, DY14 8BT
(Tel: 01299-270304)

ELLINOR HOUSE, 17 Church St, Cleobury Mortimer, DY14 8BX
(Tel: 01299-271384)

OLD BAKE HOUSE, 46-47 High Street, Cleobury Mortimer,
DY14 8DQ (Tel: 01299-270193)

TALBOT HOTEL, 29 High St, Cleobury Mortimer, DY14 8DQ
(Tel: 01299-270036)

HAMMOND COUNTRY HOTEL, Lower Street, Cleobury Mortimer,
DY14 8AA (Tel: 01299-270395)

CLEOBURY MORTIMER SERVICES

Post Office: High Street

Bank with ATM: Lloyds Bank, High Street

Visitor Information Point: Market Hall, High Street (Seasonal)

Transport connections: regular bus service 292 to Kidderminster or
Ludlow, where there are mainline railway stations.

CLEOBURY MORTIMER – LUDLOW

OS Map: Explorer 203

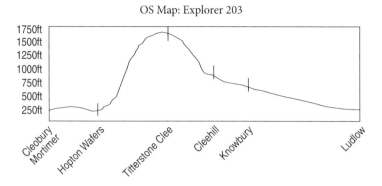

This day's walk includes the highest point on the journey at the top of Titterstone Clee, which is a few feet lower than Shropshire's highest hill, its sister Brown Clee. The day begins with a pleasant cross-country ramble away from Cleobury Mortimer, with its crooked spire waving you farewell for quite a while, then a slight descent to the pretty hamlet of Hopton Wafers before beginning the long ascent up to Titterstone Clee.

The top of Titterstone Clee, as well as giving splendid views on a clear day, has a certain spookiness in more murky weather with its abandoned mineworkers' buildings and its "golf ball" radar station. Only fitting then that you should break your journey at The Kremlin in Cleehill, whose provenance owes much to those "golf balls".

The final stretch takes you around the edge of Knowbury to join the Shropshire Way past Caynham Camp and Lower Ledwyche into the capital of the Marches, the historic town of Ludlow, nowadays known as much for its food as its turbulent past.

PLACE	DAILY MILES	TOTAL MILES
Cleobury Mortimer	–	15
Hopton Wafers	2.5	17.5
Titterstone Clee	6	21
Cleehill	8.5	23.5
Knowbury	10.5	25.5
Ludlow	14.5	29.5

CLEOBURY MORTIMER – LUDLOW
(14.5 MILES)

Cleobury Mortimer to Hopton Wafers (2.5 miles)

- Take alleyway by Talbot Hotel through car park and turn left on Childe Road then right on Love Lane past Lacon Childe School. At top of road, go left behind the Sports & Social Club to gate, then right on footpath. Where path divides past rugby pitch, go left then later left again till reaching metal gate.
- Follow footpath sign diagonally left across field to gate on minor road. Right of way is immediately opposite across field but easier to go right for forty yards then left up farm track to Lea Farm.
- As track bends into farm, go straight ahead into field and follow hedge on right to reach gap in holly hedge on right. Keep to right hedge in next field till reaching stile on right, then follow left hedge to waymarked stile and on over further stile and through gate beside reservoir site to road.
- Go right and after 20 yards take fingerposted route across large field, aiming for clump of tall trees near centre of hedge, where, taking path through new trees, find waymarked stile.
- Over stile go diagonally left across field, aiming for two trees and between trees look for waymarking on gate to right and bridge over stream.
- From bridge climb diagonally left over field to gate in far corner to left of farmhouse. Immediately through gate take waymarked stile on left and across field to further stile.
- Go across further field to bottom right corner and stile leading to right of small pool and further stile into landscaped gardens of Sproseley. Follow waymarking through gardens to gate under arch leading out to field.
- Cross field to stile into small copse and further stile on to road. Cross road and at junction take road to Hopton Wafers, passing "Botfield Chair" on right opposite gates to Hopton Court.

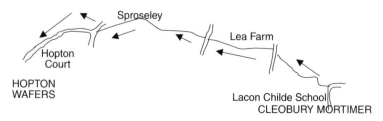

HOPTON WAFERS

Hopton Court was built in 1726 for Thomas Botfield, an important local mine-owner, who also had a reputation as a geologist and a horticulturalist. The "Botfield Chair" just outside the house gates was where the great Thomas used to sit and survey the lands around, all of which he owned. The gardens are believed to have been laid

Botfield Chair

out by Humphrey Repton and John Nash designed the verandah. The conservatory has a framework of rare Coalbrookdale ironwork.

Hopton Court is now a venue for weddings and corporate business events. In September it hosts the Hole in the Wall rock concert.

St Michael's Church, Hopton Wafers

St Michael's Church was built in 1827, though its tower predates this. It contains a remarkable memorial to Thomas Botfield, the local 19th century bigwig, and his wife Lucy. What is Lucy doing? Get the key from the cottage opposite and have a look!

The Crown at Hopton Wafers (Tel: 01299-270372), originally a 16th century coaching inn, has a high reputation for its catering, having won Shropshire Dining Pub of the Year in 2005.

Hopton Wafers to Cleehill (6 miles)

- Go through St. Michael's churchyard, with church on your right, to iron gate into field, where go left and then right on clear path to stile.
- Go left to gate and stile then right along hedge of field to just past two large oaks, where take plank bridge on right over stream and through copse to stile.
- Go ahead to stile/gate, crossing farm track, up to another gate, then head right over field to stile, followed by another field and footbridge over stream.
- Take unclear path through bracken field, aiming for right-hand oak at top of field, where go over stile and follow right edge of field to two further stiles.
- Cross field to white gate and take track through houses to road and sign for Tyglass.
- Go right, over cattle grid, then left for 300 yards on road signed Cleeton St Mary.

- Go left on stone track signposted bridleway for about half a mile, ignoring other tracks, to Ariel Cottage, where go left on steep uphill path on Magpie Hill with trees on right.
- Follow green lane winding through old quarry workings past two pools on right and, where path comes in from left go right towards farm buildings.
- Where green lane becomes stone track at Random Farm, keep straight ahead and, when fence ends, follow path towards Three-Forked Pole.
- At Pole go straight ahead over brow of hill, with Radar Station's "golf balls" clear on right, then descend to road. Go right on road up to where road doubles back and go through abandoned quarries with ruined buildings on left.
- Just past last ruins, take path on right to ridge then climb right up pathless route to trig point at top of Titterstone Clee.

THREE-FORKED POLE

Three-Forked Pole

This unusual landmark, which is replaced every 30 years, is the meeting point of three parishes. It was once upon a time the site of the beginning of the annual midsummer Titterstone Wake, when young women in their best duds joined the already-gathered young buckos and headed down a passage to drink tea made by the older women, after which things got seriously Bacchanalian.

Use your imagination! If you'd been stuck up here all year, you'd fancy some excitement too, wouldn't you?

TITTERSTONE CLEE

Titterstone Clee features on the medieval Mappa Mundi kept in Hereford Cathedral.

Its summit was the site of the largest Iron Age Hillfort in Shropshire and one of the highest in the country. Excavations show that its southern gateway and its rampart had originally been lined with timber.

In the 19th century thousands of men and their families worked in the Clee Hill quarries. Titterstone was the highest coal mine in the country then but it is more famous for the mining of dhustone, a hard rock used to build Cardiff Docks and to pave roads throughout the country.

Evidence of Victorian railways, buildings and mine workings abound.

Remains of Mine Buildings on Titterstone Clee

- Having enjoyed extensive views from summit of Titterstone Clee, retrace steps on road downhill for about one mile till reaching houses and at Hedgehog House go left on clear track past garages to stile by gate.
- Follow track, ignoring bridleway to right, past back of houses till reaching intersection with BT Premise and cattle grid on right.
- Go left on bridleway curving round to right till reaching gate into car park of Kremlin pub.
- Take footpath from front door of Kremlin to join broad track into Cleehill Village, where go right past shops, Golden Cross pub and wonderful Richard C. Swift bakery, which also has a small coffee and tearoom (nip in for fresh-made cakes and amazing selection of breads).

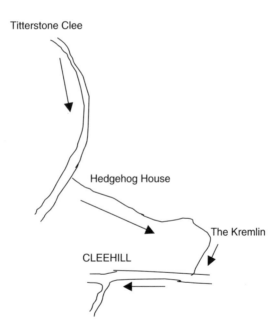

HEDGEHOG HOUSE

Hedgehog House is the HQ of the British Hedgehog Preservation Society, founded in 1982 by Major Adrian Coles to increase public awareness of the needs of our prickly friends.

The Major discovered a hedgehog trapped in the pit beneath a cattle grid, without any form of escape. He realised that without food or water the animal would die and so campaigned to have the County Council install escape ramps in all its cattle grids.

Knock on the door of Hedgehog House and ask about the Society's work, maybe even buy a little gift from their Hogalogue – a snazzy Hedgehog Mobile Phone Cover, for instance, or a Christmas Hedgehog.

Go on! Do it!

THE KREMLIN

At 1400 feet The Kremlin is Shropshire's highest pub and the second highest pub in England.

The Kremlin used to be the quarrymaster's house but it has been a pub for about 100 years.

It served the quarry workers and the local farmers, and it is still a working men's pub with darts, dominoes and quoits teams in the bar.

It owes its unusual name to the fact that, during the 1980s, it used to get Radio Moscow coming through the jukebox when there wasn't any music playing, beamed off the radio mast on top of the hill, because from here to the Urals there is no other high ground.

The Kremlin

The Kremlin (Tel: 01584-890950) is open every day except Monday from 12–11 pm, serving meals from 12–2 pm (not Mon/Tues) and Hobsons beer and Rich's Farmhouse Cider. It also offers accommodation. Stamping point at bar or, when closed, on wall outside.

Cleehill to Ludlow (6 miles)

- Opposite Golden Cross, take Tenbury road and immediately go right through kissing gate on to surfaced path, crossing two minor roads to stile into field.
- Over stile go across field, keeping to left, to further stile, then straight across next field, aiming for trees coming in from right, till reaching plank bridge and stile at bottom corner.
- Go through small field and over stile then left on to wide track descending to junction with further track coming in from right where go left to join road by Brook House.
- Go right and, ignoring footpaths and other minor roads, follow road up to crossroads at Knowbury, where go straight over.

- Shortly after passing Knowbury Hall on left, look for cottages on left and at end cottage, take path to left towards the Old Farm.
- Keep straight ahead, ignoring track left to Myrtle Cottage, through gate into field, where aim for oak tree in bottom right of field (ignoring Shropshire Way path coming in over stile on right). Go over stile, cross stream and emerge into field with lovely views of Ludlow ahead to left.
- Follow path to left by stream then round field to stile, further field and double stile, further field and stile, on to clear path (Shropshire Way sign) across field to fingerpost. Go right along hedge and cross path leading to South Farm to reach waymarked stile by gate.

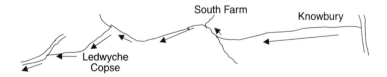

- Over stile go diagonally left, rising slightly, in direction of two isolated trees till seeing gate and stile, where go straight ahead through middle of field, with views of tree-covered Caynham Camp, till path descends right to footbridge over Cay Brook.
- Go straight ahead to stile then follow hedge on left in direction of farm buildings (superb view of Titterstone Clee to right), cross small brook and keep to low hedge on left.
- At hedge end, ignore farm track ahead (*"Private"* signs keep you out) and go left along bottom of field till entering Ledwyche Copse, where look back for last view of Titterstone Clee for a while and think of Radio Moscow!

Ledwyche Pool

- Take path through Ledwyche Copse and past Ledwyche Pool on right till reaching road by Shropshire Way sign opposite Mill House B&B, where go left.
- Follow road to bend by Little Ledwyche Farm, where go straight ahead over waymarked stile, keeping hedge on left till reaching further stile and steps up to Ludlow By-pass (Careful – very busy road!).
- Cross road and down steps to footpath round Business Park and on to Coder Road.
- At junction with Parrys Road, go right for 100 yards to Shropshire Way signpost and surfaced footpath through housing estate, crossing two roads till reaching further surfaced road, Darke Lane. Go left, then shortly afterwards right to top of Gallows Bank Millennium Green, once site of Ludlow gallows.
- Follow footpath straight down to bottom of Millennium Green and into cul-de-sac of housing estate.
- At end of cul-de-sac, go right for few yards then left into Housman Crescent and take surfaced path between privet hedges on left past back of garages, through tunnel under railway line and on to Sheet Road. Go right towards Ludlow town centre.

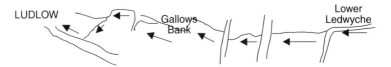

LUDLOW
Gallows Bank
Lower Ledwyche

LUDLOW PIX

Feathers Hotel

St Laurence's Church

Butter Cross

Ludlow Castle

Housman's Memorial

Broad Gate

LUDLOW STORY

'Oh, come you home on Sunday
When Ludlow's streets are still
And Ludlow's bells are calling
To farm and lane and mill.'

A.E.Housman

Ludlow is the capital of the Marches, its long history dating back to the Norman Conquest when its castle was built by Roger de Montgomery, one of William's right hand men, and its street pattern laid out. Ludlow Castle, whose shell is still a terrific sight, was the home of the Mortimers, Lords of the Marches, for many centuries and a permanent stronghold against the Welsh. Many of those Mortimers played important parts too in English history, being heavily involved on the side of the Yorkists in the Wars of the Roses, for instance, and giving a home for some time to the two young princes, Edward and Richard, sons of Edward IV, at whose death they were taken to the Tower of London to be murdered, allowing Dick Deterred to become king (*"Now is the winter of our discontent etc etc"*). Henry VII's eldest son Arthur lived in the castle with his wife Catherine of Aragon and died there but it was the creation by Henry VIII of the Council of the Marches at Ludlow that finally brought peace to the area. The town became filled with lawyers and many houses, such as The Feathers Hotel and Castle Lodge, were built as homes for Council members and their employees.

Ludlow's prosperity derived not just from its royal associations and its position as a leading place of law, but also from its long involvement in the wool trades. Until the early 17th century, selling wool, weaving cloth and making the products necessary for those involved were central occupations in Ludlow. When the wool trade declined in the 17th century, glove making took off and peaked in the early 19th century. More recently Ludlow has reinvented itself as the first Cittaslow, or "Slow City", in the United Kingdom. It is a most attractive town, with its medieval street pattern virtually intact, its many and varied old buildings, its busy market place and its splendid pubs and cafés.

Ludlow's dominant landmark is its castle, whose grounds nowadays are used for its annual Festival, when the ruins act as a wonderfully atmospheric backdrop to Shakespeare productions, and for the annual Food and Drink Fair, where local producers display their goods. It also has interesting literary associations, as Samuel Butler, the author of *Hudibras*, was Steward there in 1661 and John Milton's *Comus* was performed there for the first time in 1634.

LUDLOW CELEBRITIES

Marion de la Bruyere (12th century)

Marion de la Bruyere lived in the castle at the time of Henry II and helped her lover Arnold de Lisle, who had been imprisoned there, to escape. Marion then agreed to let her knight back into the castle for what she thought would be a nice bit of nooky. So she lowered down a rope from the high tower for him to climb up to meet her. Arnie, however had other things on his mind. Within a short time the castle was invaded by a hundred men and Ludlow was captured. Realising his betrayal, Marion grabbed Arnie's sword and cut his throat, then threw herself on to the rocks below. On quiet evenings her ghost can be seen haunting the grounds of Ludlow Castle.

The Two Princes (1470/1473–1483)

Edward and Richard, sons of Edward IV and Queen Elizabeth, lived at Ludlow Castle until, at their father's death, they were taken to the Tower of London. Here in 1483, they were murdered, allegedly by being smothered with pillows as they slept. History, and Will Shakespeare, blame the wicked Richard III but some say that Henry VII had more to gain from their deaths. We will never know.

Samuel Butler (1612–1680)

The writer Samuel Butler is said to have been composing his most famous work *Hudibras*, a satire on religious hypocrisy, in a room above the gatehouse to Ludlow Castle. Born in Worcester, Butler was appointed as Steward to oversee the refurbishing of the castle after the Civil War. He gave up his stewardship in 1662 and *Hudibras* was published in the same year. It was highly regarded by Charles II, who awarded Butler a pension of £100 per year. Lucky so-and-so!

A.E. Housman (1859–1936)

Housman is forever associated with this part of the Marches because of his long poem, full of romantic longing and melancholy, called *A Shropshire Lad*. His verses are quoted on all the tourist information ever written about the area, so it's a bit of a surprise to discover that, when he wrote *A Shropshire Lad*, he had never visited Shropshire. That's been put right now, however, as his ashes are buried at St Laurence's Church in Ludlow.

LUDLOW CAKES

EMPOROS COFFEE HOUSE, Bull Ring
Simple tearoom, tucked down a narrow passage, with home-made cakes and toasted sandwiches – try the malt and fruit loaves and coffee and walnut cake.

ARAGONS, Church Street
The home of modern "rustic " cooking, it claims. Try their award-winning honey cake with afternoon tea.

DE GREYS, Old Street
For afternoon tea in style, you can't beat it. Waitresses in black dresses and pinnies, wonderful array of teas, and scrumptious cakes.

EGO CAFÉ WINE BAR, Quality Square
Restored from an old bakery in the 1990's Ego has a continental ambience in the delightful setting of Quality Square. Live Jazz on a monthly basis.

LUDLOW ALE

WHEATSHEAF INN, Lower Broad Street
Built in 1668 and licensed as a pub in 1753, it is virtually built into the town wall. The bar is straight off the street and has a wealth of timbers and exposed stone walls. There are two beamed fireplaces which burn all winter. Serves Worthington and Bass.

CHURCH INN, Buttercross
An absolutely wonderful drinking experience made possible by welcoming staff, great local beers, very tasty and affordable pub grub. Serves Hobsons, Wye Valley, and many other Real Ales. Not to be missed!

BULL HOTEL, Bull Ring
The oldest pub in Ludlow, very central to the town and offering good choice of Real Ales, including Black Sheep and Marstons Pedigree, plus good food throughout the day. The 'Bull Yard' is tented during the summer and regularly features live bands on Fridays.

UNICORN INN, Corve Street
Décor is old and the floor and ceiling slope drastically. Beer garden by the stream is nice in the summer. Serves several Real Ales, including Timothy Taylor Landlord, London Pride and Thwaites and has excellent reputation for bar food.

LUDLOW ACCOMMODATION

WHEATSHEAF INN, Lower Broad Street, Ludlow, SY8 1PQ
(Tel: 01584-872980)

BULL HOTEL, 14 The Bull Ring, Ludlow, SY8 1AD (Tel: 01584-873611)

CECIL GUEST HOUSE, Sheet Road, Ludlow, SY8 1LR
(Tel: 01584-872442)

THE LONG HOUSE, The Sheet, Ludlow, SY8 4JT (Tel: 01584-874732)

THE MOUNT, 61 Gravel Hill, Ludlow, SY8 1QS (Tel: 01584-874084)

PALMERS HOUSE, 19 Mill Street, Ludlow, SY8 1BE (Tel: 01584-876009)

HEN & CHICKENS GUEST HOUSE, 103 Old Street, Ludlow, SY8 1NU
(Tel: 01584-874318)

ELM LODGE, Fishmore, Ludlow, SY8 3DP (Tel: 01584-872308)

HENWICK HOUSE, Gravel Hill, Ludlow, SY8 1QU (Tel: 01584-873338)

MILL HOUSE, Squirrel Lane, Ludlow, SY8 4JX (Tel: 01584-872837)

NELSON COTTAGE, Rocks Green, Ludlow, SY8 2DS
(Tel: 01584-878108)

LINNEY COTTAGE, 39 Linney, Ludlow SY8 1EE (Tel: 01584-875911)

THE WHITE HOUSE, 4 Brand Lane, Ludlow, SY8 1NN
(Tel: 01584-875592)

NUMBER TWENTY EIGHT, Lower Broad Street, Ludlow, SY8 1PQ
(Tel: 01584-875466)

LUDLOW SERVICES

Post Office: Tower Street

Banks with ATM: Lloyds, Barclays, Natwest and HSBC all in centre of town

Visitor Information Centre: Market Square (Tel: 01584-875053)

Transport connections: mainline railway station, plus bus service 192/292 from Kidderminster and Birmingham.

LUDLOW – CLUN

OS Map: Explorer 201, 203, 216 & 217

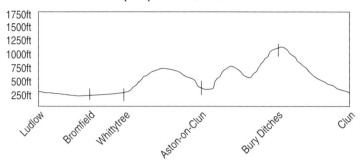

The main problem on this day's walk, apart from the distance, is having to juggle with four maps! However, that notwithstanding, there is plenty of interest as you head to the western borders of Shropshire and its boundary with Wales. Leaving Ludlow behind, its castle your companion for some way, you enter the grounds of Oakly Park leading you to the ancient settlement of Bromfield.

A cross-country stretch then takes you through the attractive Aldon and Brandhill Gutters in the Stokesay Estate and down into Broome and Aston-on-Clun with its world-renowned Arbor Tree. Both of these villages provide good luncheon opportunities (check opening times).

From Aston-on-Clun it's an uphill stretch to reach the hamlet of Kempton where you join the Shropshire Way again going past the veteran oaks of Walcot Woods, once the preserve of Clive of India. The Shropshire Way takes you then up to the wondrous viewpoint on Bury Ditches Hillfort, before your final descent into the lovely little town of Clun for an evening's carousal.

PLACE	DAILY MILES	TOTAL MILES
Ludlow	–	29.5
Bromfield	2.5	32
Whittytree	5.5	35
Aston-on-Clun	10.5	40
Bury Ditches	15	44.5
Clun	18	47.5

LUDLOW – CLUN
(18 miles)

Ludlow to Bromfield (2.5 miles)

- Leave Ludlow via road beside Ludlow Castle leading down to Dinham Bridge. Follow road over bridge bending right and at fork go right towards Cliffe Hotel. Just before reaching hotel, take kissing gate on right into field.
- Go diagonally right over field to stile/footbridge/stile in opposite corner, then follow tree-line on right over two fields with stile between, with views of Ludlow Castle to rear, Mortimer Forest to left and River Teme below to right.
- In second field, look for waymarking sign leading left to stile and down to plank bridge over brook and stile, then along line of hedge on left. After 50 yards head diagonally right across field to stile in opposite corner.

Oakly Park

- Over stile, follow same line to further stile into lane beside Priors Halton and then immediately right on to surfaced road. Follow road for over one mile through grounds of Oakly Park, looking out for Oakly Park stately home through trees on right, home of the extremely wealthy Earl of Plymouth, Robert Windsor-Clive.
- On reaching bridge over River Teme by some derelict buildings on outskirts of Bromfield, cross to briefly visit Church of St Mary and memorial to Henry Hickman.

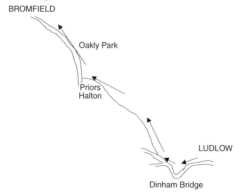

BROMFIELD

Oakly Park

Priors Halton

LUDLOW

Dinham Bridge

BROMFIELD

Once upon a time Bromfield, at the confluence of the River Onny and the River Teme, was a vast parish incorporating Ludlow and an important centre of Christian worship. St Mary's Church and the stunning gatehouse are all that remain of what was once a large Benedictine priory, dissolved, of course, in Henry VIII's time.

Priory Gatehouse

The most notable feature of the broad and dark church is the painted ceiling from 1672 above the chancel, which has been described as "the best example of the worst style of ecclesiastical art". Make of that what you will – it's certainly very unusual.

Just inside the church there is a memorial to Henry Hickman (1800-1830), the pioneer of anaesthesia who was born nearby. His discovery arose from grisly experiments he conducted to create modified animals by making

Hickman Memorial

puppies, kittens and rabbits insensible in order to amputate their limbs, from which he realised that surgical work was more easily carried out if patients had their bodies frozen by such as ether or nitrous oxide. He was ridiculed for "surgical humbug" in his lifetime.

Sounds like a nice bloke, eh?

THE COOKHOUSE/CLIVE ARMS

If you pass into the village of Bromfield, you'll come across The Cookhouse (01584-856565), or the Clive Arms as it was once known. Originally a coaching inn, it was closed in 1860 because one of the Windsor-Clives, a maiden lady, was driven back from Ludlow by a drunken coachman, who stopped at the Clive Arms rather than at Oakly Park. She demanded, and got, the closure of the inn instantly.

It remained closed till 1977 but in 2000 it was converted into an upmarket restaurant and café. The Clive coat of arms with "Audacter et Sincere" (Boldly and Sincerely) is above the fireplace.

Bromfield to Whittytree (3 miles)

- Retrace steps to Bromfield bridge over River Teme and take signposted footpath alongside river upstream from Bromfield through field, over stile and alongside amusingly-named Crawl Meadow, bending gradually away from river until merging with a wider track up to the A4113 road.
- Cross road, go through gap in hedge immediately opposite and follow hedge on right side of field boundary till reaching Cookeridge Wood, where footbridge leads to path along side of wood.
- When reaching surfaced track before Cookeridge Farm, go right for 60 yards then left over cattle grid on another surfaced track but, where track leads into farm, follow fingerposted path to right side of farm.
- Follow field boundary, ignoring stile on left, bending right till, after 100 yards, reaching footbridge in hedge on left and, after crossing, follow path straight ahead past two oak tress with brook on left.
- At next field boundary, go through gap to left then immediately right to follow field-boundary dog-legging right around field to reach (hidden) stile. Over stile go through long field with hedge on left to further (hidden) stile in hedge.
- Over stile, aim uphill to visible further stile, where go diagonally right between two oak trees towards house at Duxmoor, where there are stile and gate (Beware of Dog) leading on to road.
- Go right on road and follow till reaching road junction by telephone box at Whittytree.

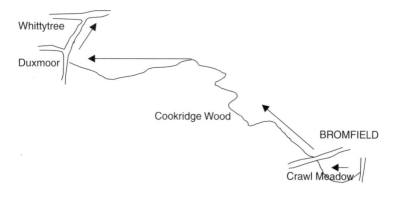

CRAWL MEADOW

Near the River Teme hereabouts there was once, according to legend, a moated mansion where lived a beautiful maiden who fell in love with a landless and penniless knight. Okay, okay, you've heard this sort of thing before but this is quite a nice variation on the old scenario. The maid, not bothered by her lover's singular lack of fortune, informed her father that the marriage was to take place the following morning at St Mary's Church in Bromfield. Well, what's the point of being the father of a beautiful maiden if you can't make life a bit difficult for her? So Lord Bountiful pronounced that, if she went ahead with the marriage, her dowry would only be as much land as she could crawl between sunset and sunrise. Donning a pair of leather breeches, the maid astonished everyone by crawling four miles before sunrise. Her father, who wasn't such a mean old stick after all, was so impressed he made her his only heiress and the lands remained in her family for many generations after.

Does your heart good to hear of the toffs behaving decently, doesn't it?

WERNLAS RARE CHICKEN COLLECTION

Sue and Shaun Hammon have been keeping chickens for fifty years and the Wernlas collection is an internationally acclaimed conservation centre, providing a vital gene pool for rare and traditional breeds of chicken. Wernlas is open every day except Monday from 10.30 am to 5.30 pm. If you've got time, you might choose to call in and consider purchasing a chicken for yourself so you've always got a supply of fresh eggs.

Rare breed poultry

Choose from the amazing variety on offer here. Fancy a Rhode Island Red, a Black Cochin or a Buff Sussex? Maybe you'd rather have a Black Leghorn or Sicilian Buttercup. You can choose a hen that produces brown eggs, one that lays sky-blue eggs, or one that lays cream eggs (no, not those with chocolate outside them!).

Whittytree to Aston-on-Clun (5 miles)

- By telephone box at Whittytree, take signed footpath through derelict farm buildings and follow path alongside Stonehouse pools to enter woodland through gate.
- Follow path (listening out for Wernlas Rare Chicken collection) contouring round valley on Brandon Gutter, keeping stream close on right, over two stiles, where footpath becomes blue-signed bridleway till reaching metal gate into field.
- Follow right edge of field on path to reach thatched Brandy Bottom Cottage, where go left on broad ascending track to reach surfaced road at Brandhill Farm.
- Go right and, at fork in road, go left, following contours till reaching dogleg in road by Goat Hill. Go right 10 yards on bridleway then left through gate and diagonally across field, aiming for blue-taped fence.
- Continue straight across field to gate in hedge, where go left on surfaced track leading to Roman Road (once the main thoroughfare known as Watling Street South between Roman camps at Leintwardine and Wroxeter – imagine those legions walking with you).
- Go right and at crossroads go left past Rowton Manor and, after crossing B4367 and under railway bridge, into Broome, where there is a station for trains to Shrewsbury and Swansea and an appropriately-named pub, Engine and Tender (01588-660275).
- Continue on road to reach Aston-on-Clun and Kangaroo Inn, with shop and Post Office next door.

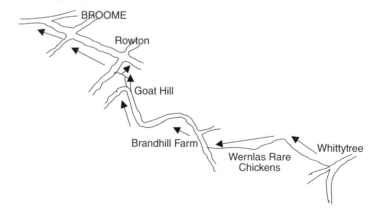

ASTON-ON-CLUN

BROOME

Rowton

Goat Hill

Brandhill Farm

Wernlas Rare Chickens

Whittytree

ASTON-ON-CLUN

Aston-on-Clun is an attractive Shropshire village which is unique for celebrating Arbor Day. Every year on 29th May, villagers decorate with flags a black poplar tree (very rare in England) that stands in the middle of the village and there is a pageant led by a mock bride and groom to this tree, followed by dancing and other such frolics. The ceremony, a relic of prehistoric superstitions, dates back to the Restoration when the newly-installed Charles II declared May 29th as a national holiday (which also happened to be his birthday, so he would be drunk as a skunk anyway).

This became known as Oak Apple Day, in memory of the oak tree Charlie had hidden in to escape his pursuers, and villages dressed up trees and joined in the revelry with a knees-up and much drinking. In Aston-on-Clun, it became known as Arbor Day.

Arbor Tree

The tradition died out in most places but in Aston-on-Clun it has continued, largely due to he generosity of Squire John Marston who married Mary Sibdon on Arbor Day in 1786, arrived at the Arbor tree and saw the villagers having a good time, and set up a trust fund to pay for the care of the tree and the flags. In 1995 the 300-year old Arbor tree fell down in a storm and was replaced by a 20-year old sapling taken from the old tree.

THE KANGAROO INN

The Kangaroo Inn

The unusually-named Kangaroo Inn (01588-660263) dates back to the 1830s. Then an enterprising local builder bought some timbers from the S.S. Kangaroo, an ocean-going ship that had passed its sell-by date and was being broken up at Pembroke Docks. He shipped them here and built the pub with them.

Open every lunchtime except Monday and Tuesday from 12 – 2 pm for good food and excellent Real Ales from the Wye Valley brewery and Hobsons.

Stamping point at bar or, when closed, on outside wall.

Aston-on-Clun to Bury Ditches (4.5 miles)

- From Kangaroo Inn follow road to left, passing Arbor Tree, till just before end of village, where footpath sign takes you on broad track to right and, at intersection of paths after 50 yards, go left.
- Follow this track to gate at junction of paths, where take stile opposite on to gradual ascent in field beside overgrown tree-lined path.
- Enter woodland at gate with Welcome sign and continue climbing till path levels out in clearing and look for tree on left with FP painted on.
- Follow path to right along edge of wood descending to junction of paths at bottom of hill, where go right for 30 yards then, by PAT sign on tree, look for stile in dip and cross field diagonally to planks over stream and gap in fence.
- Continue on diagonal line uphill to further stile, then short sharp climb to ridge and look for waymarked stile on right at edge of woodland.
- Follow path through trees, maintaining height, to opposite edge of woodland, then over stile and through opposite gate into field, where follow field boundary through several fields to reach road at Kempton.
- Turn right and look for Shropshire Way sign down farm track to left by sign for Kempton Farm at edge of village. Almost immediately go right through gates and cross field to stile, where go left across bridge (Restored 2002) on surfaced track past house to stile on left.
- Follow Shropshire Way signs around left edge of field to two stiles and broad junction of lanes, where go right and follow broad track bending left past disused quarries and Lodge Farm to enter Walcot Wood.
- Take track forking left past cottages and follow through edge of woods to reach Stanley Cottage and up to road. Go right and, at sign for Jack Mytton Way, go left into picnic area and follow signs through picnic benches to climb up to gate into ancient Bury Ditches hillfort.

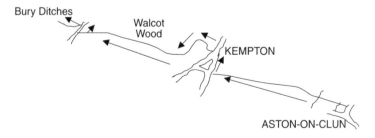

WALCOT WOOD

Walcot Wood, now managed by the National Trust, was once part of the 18,000 acre Walcot estate owned by Clive of India, who made his money by some dodgy dealings in India. The estate was originally an Elizabethan deer park and its unique situation in a secluded valley, protected from extremes of weather and pollution, has meant that it is the home of some very ancient oak trees. Oak trees reputedly spend 300 years growing, 300 years resting and 300 years gradually dying. In this last stage they are known as veteran trees and you'll pass several as

Veteran Oak Tree

you walk. They are home to rare species of lichen and beetles.

Clive bought the Walcot estate in 1763 and immediately set about developing the existing Tudor house into a grand Georgian manor, designed by the leading architect of his day. Walcot Hall remained in the Clive family for 170 years but then in 1929 it was sold to a toilet manufacturer from the Black Country. It is now used for posh weddings and corporate knees-ups.

How are the mighty fallen, eh?

BURY DITCHES

Bury Ditches Hillfort

Bury Ditches hillfort is only visible because of a freak of nature. Until 1976, it was covered in trees but then a fortuitous storm blew most of them down and the site was cleared by the Forestry Commission to reveal the magnificent outlines of this ancient fortification.

This oval fort would originally have housed several farmsteads and their occupants, banding together for mutual protection.

Go through the "inturned entrance" and climb up to the toposcope for spectacular views of the Clee Hills, Wenlock Edge, Stiperstones, the Long Mynd, the neolithic axe factory of Corndon Hill and the Clun forest.

Bury Ditches to Clun (3 miles)

- Take main path through hillfort and after 20 yards, go right to toposcope for amazing views.
- From toposcope, go left on fort rampart to reach gate/stile, where follow track to right around edge of fort downhill till reaching T-junction, where go left (or end up going round in circles).
- Broad forest track leads downhill to join with Jack Mytton Way coming in from left.
- On reaching fork in paths with fingerpost signposted Clun, take left fork descending out of forest till reaching junction of paths by isolated house, advertising eggs for sale (N.B. views of Clun nestling in the valley below left).
- Take signposted right track through Guilden Down Farm buildings to join road descending left after farm (watch out for distinctive Clun Forest sheep in this area).
- After half mile look for stile, waymarked Shropshire Way, in hedge on right.
- Cross two fields with stiles between to reach further stile and path around Mill Barn Cottage to rejoin road.
- Go right and follow road past Youth Hostel into centre of Clun.

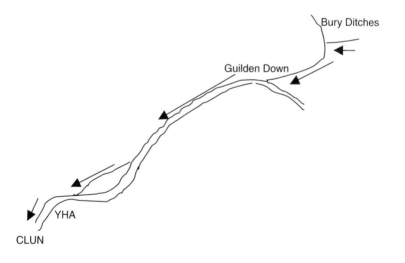

CLUN FOREST SHEEP

Clun Forest sheep have been nibbling the grass and producing lambs in this region for close on 1000 years. Originally tended by semi-nomadic shepherds in the huge expanse that was known as Clun Forest, they can now be found in many other parts of the world as well.

Over the past 80 years the breed has retained all the positive attributes which has made it popular worldwide. However, the ears are now carried slightly higher and the face is of a darker shade of brown. The fleece of Clun Forest sheep is generally of a high quality, and is popular with knitters and for making futons.

Since the Clun Forest Sheep Society's formation in 1925, the Clun Forest breed has spread from the ancient kingdom of Mercia all over the UK and Ireland. They have also been exported throughout Europe, Africa and North America. Clun Forest sheep are known as a breed for all seasons.

CLUN PIX

Clun Bridge

Trinity Hospital and Almshouses

Clun Castle

St George's Church

Clun Museum

John Osborne's Tombstone

CLUN STORY

"Clunton and Clunbury, Clungunford and Clun,
Are the quietest places under the sun."

A.E. Housman

You may never want to leave the idyllic town of Clun. As its name suggests, it is a very ancient British settlement which grew in Saxon times around its church because of its position on the droving road from Wales to London. At the time of the Norman Conquest, Clun belonged to Wild Edric whose revolt against William was put down, resulting in his lands being given to Norman lords. One of them, Picot de Say, built Clun Castle and the grid pattern of the town was established by the Normans on the north side of the 14th century Clun Bridge, leaving the Saxon settlement on the south side. A local saying is that *"whoever crosses Clun Bridge comes back sharper than he went"* (whatever that means).

The attractive stone-built Trinity Hospital was founded in 1618 by Henry Howard, Earl of Northampton, who had by then inherited the Barony of Clun. The hospital is actually almshouses, originally for twelve old men of good character to spend their sunset days, but now occupied by men and women. Howard's reasons for establishing these almshouses were widely believed to be because of his guilt over his involvement in the Thomas Overbury Affair. Howard's neice, Frances, in seeking to escape from a loveless marriage, sought to poison her husband but her plot was discovered by the said Overbury. Uncle Henry then arranged for him to be locked in the Tower and subsequently poisoned. The almshouses were built shortly afterwards. Draw your own conclusions.

Clun has been the inspiration for writers who have visited. Sir Walter Scott stayed at the Buffalo Inn while writing *The Betrothed*, which features a castle known as the Garde Doloreuse based on the ruined Clun Castle. In E.M. Forster's *Howard's End*, the village of Clun is called Oniton. And the English playwright John Osborne spent his latter years living here, his gravestone being in St. George's churchyard.

Nowadays Clun is a haven of peace and calm, largely cut off from the modern world, and with a wealth of lovely old buildings. Worth mentioning is its unusual and probably unique Green Man Festival, held over the May Day weekend every year. The Green Man leaf mask has been around for centuries, a symbol of the union of mankind and nature, and the remnant of primitive fertility worship. The festival features a mock battle between the Green Man and the Frost Queen enacted on Clun Bridge and it attracts large numbers of visitors for the weekend.

CLUN CELEBRITIES

Henry Howard, Earl of Northampton (1540–1614)

Henry Howard was a Roman Catholic intriguer at the time of Elizabeth I and of James I, known for treachery. He was imprisoned on several occasions for his dalliance with Mary, Queen of Scots. On Elizabeth's death, he successfully sought to influence the new king, James I, and gained honours and favours. He was one of the judges in the trials of Sir Walter Raleigh and of Guy Fawkes but is best remembembered now for his involvement in the Overbury Affair.

John Osborne (1929–1994)

John Osborne is often credited with having changed the face of English theatre with his 1956 play, *Look Back in Anger*. Its central character, Jimmy Porter, portrayed the rebellious nature of the post-war generation and came to represent the 'Angry Young Men'. Osborne also wrote the screen play for the film version of *Tom Jones*. His later writing, however, although prolific, never matched the promise of his early work and he retired to live in the tranquillity of Clun.

Wild Edric (11th century)

Edric owned much land in the Welsh Marches around the Clun area at the time of the Norman Conquest. He submitted to William the Conqueror in 1066 but when some of William's mates started pillaging in Edric's territories, he declared war on them and regained his lands. Later, however, he appears to have made peace with the king but then revolted again, was captured and, allegedly, imprisoned in a cave below Stiperstones. According to legend, Edric leads a Wild Hunt of flaming-eyed dogs, that appears whenever England is threatened by foreign invasion. Allegedly, anyone who witnesses the Wild Hunt will be punished by death or madness!

CLUN CAKES

BRIDGE COFFEE SHOP, Church Street
Friendly tearoom selling home-made cakes, sandwiches, pasties, and scones. Welcomes *"walkers with muddy boots"*.

THE MALTINGS CAFÉ, High Street
Building is an old malt house, popular with ramblers, cyclists, locals, families, farmers, holidaymakers – a haven of old-fashioned charm and good food in a wonderful setting.

CLUN ALE

WHITE HORSE INN, The Square
Traditional inn with log fires, serving very good food and an excellent range of Real Ales (a passion of the landlord), including Hobsons, Woods, Wye Valley, Salopian, John Roberts, plus Weston's Cider, and is always in the CAMRA guide.

SUN INN, 10 High Street
15th century inn serving good food and Real Ales, including Banks's, Hobsons and Marstons. Look for the 16th century wallpaper and the gravestone flag floor.

BUFFALO INN, The Square
Old stone pub with lots of beams and hops, allegedly where Walter Scott stayed. Currently closed.

CLUN ACCOMMODATION

WHITE HORSE INN, The Square, Clun, SY7 8JA (Tel: 01588-640305)

SUN INN, High Street, Clun, SY7 8JB (Tel: 01588-640559)

CROWN HOUSE, Church Street, Clun, SY7 8JW (Tel: 01588-640780)

CLUN FARM HOUSE, High Street, Clun, SY7 8JB
(Tel: 01588-640432)

THE MILL YHA, Clun, SY7 8NY (Tel: 01588-640582 or 01568-620517
for bookings more than 7 days in advance)

CLUN SERVICES

Post Office: Church Street

Bank with ATM: in Clun Post Office (open 9.00–5.30 Mon–Sat)

Visitor Information Point: Clun Garage, High Street
(Tel: 01588-640220)

Transport connections: nearest station is Craven Arms but taxi and bus
services very rare.

CLUN – BISHOP'S CASTLE

OS Map: Explorer 201 & 216

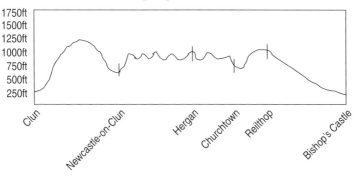

Welcome to one of the most spectacular day's of your journey, much of it on that ancient boundary between England and Wales, Offa's Dyke, here in all its glory still evident and stunning some 1200 years after it was built. Firstly, however, you need to gain your height with a pleasant and gradual climb out of Clun and up to Springhill Farm, where you join the Offa's Dyke Path as it sweeps down the hillside towards Newcastle-on-Clun. If you leave Clun late, you should be able to get refreshments here from its shop or the Crown Inn, but be warned: there are no other services before Bishop's Castle.

After leaving Newcastle-on-Clun your route takes you on the switchback section of the Offa's Dyke Path, where it's hard to get into a rhythm but where you have to admire the power of Offa to organise the building of this Dyke on these hills. At Hergan there's a chance to catch your breath but nothing else, then it's up and down again to reach Churchtown, where you leave Offa's earthwork to take the more gentle Shropshire Way through rolling countryside till you get to the lovely old town of Bishop's Castle with its two microbreweries – bliss!

PLACE	DAILY MILES	TOTAL MILES
Clun	–	47.5
Newcastle-on-Clun	4.5	52
Hergan	6.5	54
Churchtown	8	55.5
Reilthop	10.5	58
Bishop's Castle	14	61.5

CLUN-BISHOP'S CASTLE
(14 miles)

Clun to Newcastle-on-Clun (4.5 miles)

- Take Knighton road out of Clun past St George's Church then second road on right, signposted Springhill and Anchor.
- Just past St George's Place take signed footpath on left and after 50 yards go through kissing gate on right to rising path with trees on either side, eventually bending right behind isolated cottage down to join road at Pear Tree Cottage, where go left.
- Follow road, still climbing, until shortly after passing Cymfrydd Farm reaching crossroads, where go right (signposted Springhill and Anchor) then almost immediately left on Jack Mytton Way, surfaced bridleway towards Burfield Farm.
- Go through Burfield Farm buildings and after 200 yards, at signpost for Jack Mytton Way to left, go straight ahead to two metal gates and go through right-hand gate.
- Go diagonally right uphill across field to twin metal gates in opposite corner, then continue climbing to further metal gate (N.B. Offa's Dyke is straight ahead here). Climb diagonally right to gate, continuing to further gate on right of Springhill Farm to road.
- Cross road and go over stile on Offa's Dyke Path, descending to further stile and DEFRA sign, then follow left field edge to stile leading to wide track with Dyke on right.
- At junction of paths go left and follow track as it bends right downhill through farm buildings of Lower Spoad. Then go left on road into Newcastle-on-Clun for shop and Crown Inn.

NEWCASTLE-ON-CLUN

THE CROWN INN

The Crown Inn, which also incorporates the village shop, is a freehouse serving a range of Real Ales, including Hobsons and John Roberts, and pub grub. It is a traditional country pub with unusual little window seats and stunning scenery all around. Darts and dominoes available, if you have the energy. It also offers accommodation.

The Crown Inn

Open daily from 12–2 pm for food. (Tel: 01588-640271)

Stamping point at bar or, when closed, at shop next door.

NEWCASTLE-ON-CLUN

The Church of St John the Evangelist is probably the major feature of the tiny village of Newcastle-on-Clun. It has a most unusual revolving lych gate to lead you into its churchyard.

St John's Church

On the river bank to the south-east of the village is the motte of what was once a Norman castle. On the hill above is the Iron Age hillfort of Fron Camp.

From the churchyard you can see Offa's Dyke snaking up the hillside opposite.

Newcastle-on-Clun to Churchtown (3.5 miles)

- Take road to right just past The Crown and follow, passing school, to T-junction. Go right, passing St John's Church and road to left, to rejoin Offa's Dyke Path by steps on left leading to two stiles and sharp climb.
- Go over brow of hill then short descent to stile and further sharp ascent to brow of Graig Hill and stile, leading to clear path descending to meet track from Bridge Farm on right and stile into field.
- Follow path going right across field to stile and footbridge then stile on to surfaced lane at Mardu, where go right and after 30 yards at junction go left and immediately right at sign for Lower Mount.
- Go past cottage and through metal gate and take right fork in paths on to Dyke rising through woodland, then descending slightly by marker post before climbing again to stile and 122 wooden steps (count them!).
- Further stile leads to clear sheep track rising more gradually to stile and surfaced lane at Hergan. Catch your breath then cross road and over further stile to fingerpost, where Shropshire Way joins Offa's Dyke Path.
- Take lower of two paths to left and follow Dyke on well waymarked path on this switchback over several stiles to reach Corvedale Crisis Care Centre at Middle Knuck.
- Go over stile, cross Centre's access road and look for marker post back to the Offa's Dyke Path. Follow over more stiles to reach surfaced lane.
- Go straight across lane to stile and continue to woodland, where descend on partially stepped path sharply to Churchtown.

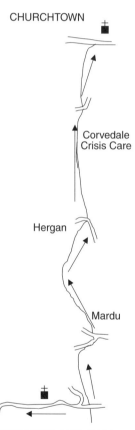

CHURCHTOWN

Corvedale
Crisis Care

Hergan

Mardu

NEWCASTLE-ON-CLUN

OFFA'S DYKE

Offa's Dyke

Offa was king of Mercia from A.D. 759 to 796 who united all of the Anglo-Saxon tribes south of the Humber by defeating them in battle. He built his mighty earthwork, stretching "from sea to sea", in order to create a boundary between his kingdom and that of the Welsh. It is an amazing creation and 60 to 70 miles of it are still clearly evident.

The Offa's Dyke Path follows the line of the Dyke from its beginning above the Severn Estuary just south of Chepstow for 177 miles to its ending in Prestatyn in North Wales.

"Special Offa", by the author of this guide, is a highly rewarding account of walking this path. Buy it!

CHURCHTOWN

Churchtown is a church without a town, its main settlement being Mainstone just down the valley. "Maen" in Welsh means a stone, so this place is really Stonestone. The stone about which all the fuss is made sits on the floor of the church by the pulpit. It is believed that once upon a time this place was a trading post where the Welsh and the English would do business. The stone was used as a weight to measure 200 pounds of grain (plus 4.5 pounds for the bag!).

The Mainstone

Churchtown to Bishop's Castle (6 miles)

- Just before completing descent through woodland into Churchtown, go right at fingerpost for Shropshire Way on short ascent to stile on to path through Churchtown Wood to reach stile on to surfaced lane, where go left to junction at Cow Pasture Gate.
- Go right and after 30 yards take stile in hedge on right on to clear path over field climbing to successive stiles on to forest track in Knuck Wood, descending to stile at road by Reilth Farm. Go left over River Unk to next road junction.
- At junction go straight ahead over stile through light woodland to metal gate, then go left on stony path rising through field to metal gate at top of field.
- Go on to green lane and follow through several gates, passing modern house at Fron, to reach gate on to road at Vron Farm at Reilthtop.

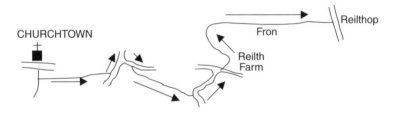

- Go left and after 20 yards right through gate past farm buildings to further gate.
- Follow path around left side of field bending eventually to reach stile by gate, with wonderful views of Corndon Hill, Stiperstones, Long Mynd and Bishop's Castle nestling in valley.
- Go diagonally right across field to metal gate and path beyond descending past edge of Henley Wood to reach metal gate to surfaced lane.
- Go right through Middle Woodbatch Farm grounds (centre for horse-riding) on track that becomes surfaced lane.

- At Wood House follow road on Z-bend and, immediately after crossing stream, take stile in hedge on right on to meadow path.
- Follow line of stream through several fields with stiles between.
- At rusty metal gate by sheep pen, do not take stile right into Colebatch but go left uphill, with old quarry on left, to stile.
- Follow right field edge over further stiles to gate by Field Cottage leading into Field Lane.
- At end of Field Lane, go right on Church Lane and follow past Fire Station to reach Six Bells pub at bottom of Church Street in Bishop's Castle.

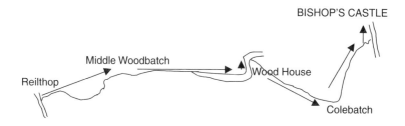

BISHOP'S CASTLE PIX

House on Crutches

Railway Museum

Poppy House Tearooms

Three Tuns Brewery

Six Bells Brewery Tap

St John's Church

BISHOP'S CASTLE STORY

"There it shone, its clustered roofs, square church tower and miniature railway station all sloping up a hill with the inconsequence of a card house. Beyond were meadows, steep woods, blue distance, smoke-coloured hills, and more hills so pale as to fade on the sky."

Mary Webb

There aren't any bishops in Bishop's Castle nowadays, nor is there much visible of any castle. The town was originally a Saxon settlement but was given to the Bishops of Hereford by its Saxon lord, Egwin Shakehead, in thanks for having been cured of the palsy at Hereford Cathedral. The Normans built their borderland castle on the hill top in the 11th century and the town's grid pattern was laid out below the castle shortly afterwards. The castle itself fell into disrepair in the 16th century, the present-day Castle Hotel now occupying its site, while its bowling green was once the castle keep.

Bishop's Castle has little prominence in national history, although it was famous for being a "rotten borough", sending two MPs to parliament for many years and on one occasion sending four, because they each got the same number of votes. Until 1967, Bishop's Castle was the smallest borough in England.

The Bishop's Castle Railway was one of the most eccentric inventions in England. It ran for 10 miles through tiny villages between the town and Craven Arms and was originally intended to continue to Montgomery. It never made money and for most of its existence was in receivership. On one occasion bailiffs tore up the rails because a local bigwig was owed money, but the bailiffs were persuaded to go to the local pub, while the locals replaced the rails and waved a train through. The line closed in 1935 but there is a Railway Museum in the town where its hilarious story is told.

Also worthy of a visit is the curiously-named House on Crutches Museum at the top of the High Street and, for all Real Ale lovers, Bishop's Castle's two microbreweries, attached respectively to The Three Tuns and The Six Bells pubs. The Church of St John the Baptist has a typically squat border tower, though the rest of it was rebuilt in Victorian times.

The town, despite its relative isolation from the rest of the world, is a really thriving community, which seems to have maintained its old structures and customs at the same time as welcoming newcomers (and new housing) into its environs. It has become one of my favourite places.

BISHOP'S CASTLE CELEBRITIES

Bishops of Hereford

It's all a long time ago but Bishop's Castle was under the control of the Bishops of Hereford from the 8th century, when Egwin Shakehead experienced his miracle cure, until the second half of the 16th century when the bishops handed the town over to Elizabeth I. Little is known about individual bishops and how much they were involved in the administration of the town, or even if they ever visited, though a Bishop Swinfield in the late 13th century is recorded as having *"eaten the good people out of house and home"*. From the looks of the pictures I've seen, the bishops certainly enjoyed their Real Ales, bought no doubt from The Three Tuns or The Six Bells.

Todley Tum (18th century)

Todley Tum was what used to be known as a 'conjuror' but what we might call a fortune-teller. People would go to him and press some money on him in return for information about some upcoming event, such as a cock-fight or the prospects of making a match with a local maiden or young man. One story tells of a farmer who went to ask Tom if he would be called up to join the army. After he'd told him his fortune, Tom asked the farmer how he wanted to go home – high, low or level. When the farmer chose high, he found himself flying above the trees till he dropped down into his farmyard.

Louis Paces (?–1814)

A tombstone near the belfry door of St. John the Baptist's church bears the legend: "A là memoire de Louis Paces, Lieut.-Colonel de Chevaux legers, chevalier des ordres militaires des deux Siciles et d'Espayne". This unusual inscription records the death of one of the French soldiers imprisoned here at Bishop's Castle at the time of the Peninsular Wars, though little else is known of him.

Richard Gifford (1725–1807)

Born in Bishop's Castle, Richard Gifford achieved fame as a poet and theologian. His best-known poem was *Contemplation*, which begins thus:

Verse sweetens toil, however rude the sound;
She feels no biting pang the while she sings;
Nor, as she turns the giddy wheel around,
Revolves the sad vicissitudes of things.

Gripping, isn't it?

BISHOP'S CASTLE CAKES

POPPY HOUSE, Market Square (Closed Tues)
Daytime menu includes home-made Shropshire Lasagne, Leicestershire Stilton Potato Cake, Pine Nuts & Pesto Tagliatelle and sandwiches.

CAPRICHO, High Street (Closed Wed)
Friendly café and delicatessen serving good home-made food, including freshly-made sandwiches, hot paninis, mediterranean deli snacks and home-made cakes. Tea, coffee, hot chocolate all fair-traded.

VICTORIA'S CAFÉ, New Street
Popular and friendly café selling home-made cakes and snacks with daily specials.

BISHOP'S CASTLE ALE

SIX BELLS, Church Street
Traditional old pub full of charm and character with big stone fireplace and log burner. No music played anywhere in the pub. Good, hearty food with some unusual dishes. Sells four of its own Real Ales – Big Nev, Cloud Nine, Old Recumbent, Marathon, all served to perfection.

THREE TUNS, Salop Street
Look for the Victorian brew tower in the yard. The walk-in fireplace with barrels above is a particular attraction, as is the beamed ceiling. Ever-changing menu of good food and sells its own John Roberts Real Ales. Occasional jazz evenings.

BOAR'S HEAD HOTEL, Church Street
One of the earliest surviving buildings in Bishop's Castle with a wealth of exposed beams and a welcoming log fire. Serves good food and Courage beers.

CROWN & ANCHOR VAULTS, High Street
Popular with the local young people with regular music nights.

CASTLE HOTEL, Market Square
A large country town hotel set up a steep drive. No music inside the pub. Huge beer garden with great views over the town. Serves good food but can be pricey. Serves Hobsons and Bass Real Ales.

BISHOP'S CASTLE ACCOMMODATION

CASTLE HOTEL, The Square, Bishop's Castle, SY9 5BN
(Tel: 01588-638403)

BOARS HEAD HOTEL, Church Street, Bishop's Castle, SY9 5AE
(Tel: 01588-638521)

MAGNOLIA, 3 Montgomery Road, Bishop's Castle, SY9 5EZ
(Tel: 01588-638098)

OLD BRICK GUEST HOUSE, 7 Church Street, Bishop's Castle, SY9 5AA
(Tel: 01588-638471)

OLD TIME, 29 High Street, Bishop's Castle, SY9 5BE
(Tel: 01588-638467)

POPPY HOUSE, 20 Market Square, Bishop's Castle, SY9 5BN
(Tel: 01588-638443)

PORCH HOUSE, High Street, Bishop's Castle, SY9 5BE
(Tel: 01588-638854)

CLAREMONT, Bull Lane, Bishop's Castle, SY9 5BW
(Tel: 01588-638170)

BISHOP'S CASTLE SERVICES

Post Office: High Street

Banks with ATM: HSBC and Barclays in High Street

Visitor Information Point: Old Time, High Street (Tel: 01588-638467)

Transport connections: regular 552/553 bus service to Shrewsbury.

BISHOP'S CASTLE – CHURCH STRETTON

OS Map: Explorer 216 & 217

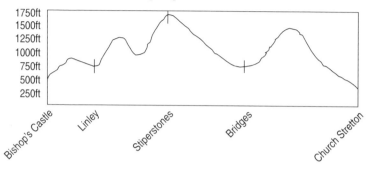

Another spectacular day's walking takes you to the heart of Shropshire's Area of Outstanding Natural Beauty over the heather-clad, bilberry-strewn, mystical and magical Shropshire hills. Once out of Bishop's Castle, you take the Shropshire Way route through the ancient settlements of Lydham, More and Linley before you commence your ascent of Linley Hill with its wonderful beech avenue.

A brief descent brings you to the start of your major climb up to the rocky outcrops of the Stiperstones, site of many legends and the inspiration to writers. A steady descent from there brings you to The Horsehoe Inn at Bridges for well-earned refreshment.

Then, leaving the Shropshire Way and joining the Jack Mytton Way, there's one more climb up and over the bleak moorland on top of Long Mynd before descending on Motts Road to Carding Mill Valley, favourite spot for generations of picnicking families, and into Church Stretton, sometimes known as *"Little Switzerland"*, to sample the delights of its cafés and bars.

PLACE	DAILY MILES	TOTAL MILES
Bishop's Castle	–	61.5
Linley	3	64.5
Stiperstones	6.5	68
Bridges	10	71.5
Church Stretton	15	76.5

BISHOP'S CASTLE – CHURCH STRETTON
(15 miles)

Bishop's Castle to Linley (3 miles)

- Leave Bishop's Castle via Bull Street beside Castle Hotel and at T-junction go left into Bull Lane, then right into Castle Green, where a fingerpost for Shropshire Way points to a path between cottages.
- Find gate leading to well-defined path to gate, continuing uphill to two successive stiles on to brow of hill (N.B. rocky outcrops of Stiperstones visible ahead in middle distance).
- Follow path to further stile in corner of field, then straight across next field and, with copse on left, descend to stile on to B4385 road.
- Go right on road for 200 yards to Upper Hebeland Farm, where take stile to waymarked path (may be overgrown) diagonally across field to find fingerpost.
- Follow direction of fingerpost along left field becoming clear path between hedge and fence then into new plantation of trees to reach metal gate.
- Through gate continue downhill to gate on to wide farm track at bottom, going right to reach A488, where go left for 300 yards into Lydham (N.B. good shop for provisions etc).
- From Lydham & More Village Hall car park, take stile at top left corner and go diagonally left across field to further stile, then continue on same line across next field, to left of large oak, to plank bridge and stile.
- Cross next field through earth remains of motte and bailey castle to find gate in hedge on to surfaced lane with More village and church to right.
- Go through gate opposite and take path across three fields with stiles between them to reach surfaced lane. Go left to Linley Hall.

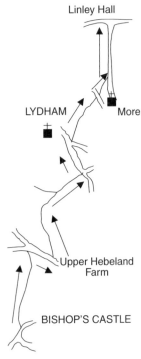

LYDHAM

Hard to believe now but Lydham was a town in Anglo-Saxon times. Nowadays it is little more than a group of houses around the church, plus a shop.

The Church of the Holy Trinity was originally built in the 13th century, restored in 1642 and largely rebuilt in 1885.

The Lydham Oak in the grounds of nearby Lydham Manor is one of the largest oak trees in the country, measuring 30 feet around its girth.

Holy Trinity Church

MORE

The picturesque village of More, with its timber-framed houses, would once have housed the families that serviced the More family of nearby Linley Hall. It was not the home of Oliver Twist!

More Rectory

The village surrounds St Peter's Church whose squat tower is similar to that of St George's Church in Clun.

The motte and bailey earthworks would once have been the Norman More Castle.

LINLEY

Linley is little more than a few houses dominated by the Palladian mansion of Linley Hall, which was built in 1742 by Henry Joynes, comptroller of works at Blenheim Palace. The site, however, has been the home of the More family since the Norman Conquest.

Robert More, who commissioned the building of the Hall, was an 18th century botanist and a friend of Linnaeus. He is credited with introducing larch trees to England.

Linley Hall

Linley to Stiperstones (3.5 miles)

- At road junction in front of Linley Hall go right and follow road to next road junction, where go left climbing on surfaced lane signposted Cold Hill and The Bog.
- At top of hill, just before road forks, go right on signposted path, still climbing to reach wooden gate, leading to lovely track through Linley Beeches avenue.
- Path goes through metal gates till reaching brow of Linley Hill, where splendid views of Corndon Hill to left and Stiperstones ahead can be seen.
- Follow path over brow of hill to further gate, then gradually descend, bending to left through two further gates. At second gate begin sharp descent with fence and copse on left to reach stile, then continue descent to metal gate on to surfaced lane to left of Ridge Farm. Go right.
- Follow lane bending left than right and at brow of hill look for signposted path descending through woodland to stile and footbridge over stream. Climb through next field aiming for plank bridge then to right of stone cottage for stile into lane.
- Go right and almost immediately left on signposted track climbing through more woodland till, near rocky outcrop, reaching junction of paths in land where trees have been cleared in order to reintroduce heather to hilltop.
- Go right through cleared land to reach stile and clearer footpath leading to gate and shortly afterwards to stile and path through woodland.
- When path emerges at stile into field, go forward over field, heading towards rocky outcrops of Stiperstones, and reach stile on to road, where cross to enter Stiperstones National Nature Reserve through gate.

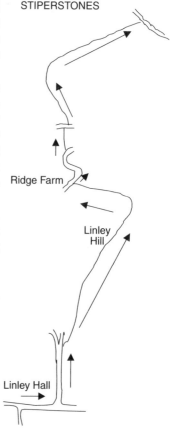

STIPERSTONES

Ridge Farm

Linley
Hill

Linley Hall

LINLEY BEECHES

The Linley Beeches avenue is believed to date back to the time of the Napoleonic Wars, possibly planted by unemployed ex-soldiers. Its design owes much to the fashion of the time among wealthy landowners to create spectacular landscapes, often with non-native trees, and Linley Beeches certainly is that.

The beech is native to Britain but is more commonly found in the south of England. Many of the older trees are now dying but replacement saplings are growing alongside them so that this feature of the landscape will remain for many years.

Linley Beeches

STIPERSTONES

Stiperstones is a nationally-important geological site with its stone-jagged ridge being a remnant of the Ice Age. The heathland around it is home to curlew, red grouse, skylark, meadow pipit, stonechat and whinchat. It also produces bilberries, crowberries and cowberries. The "Back to Purple" project, mounted by English Nature, Shropshire Wildlife Trust and Forest Enterprise, is gradually restoring the heathland around the ridge by felling conifers and encouraging the spread of heather by destroying bracken.

Stiperstones

Stiperstones to Bridges (3.5 miles)

- From sign for Stiperstones National Nature Reserve, follow ascending path past several outcrops of rock to reach Cranberry Rock then Manstone Rock with trig point on top.
- Continue on broad, ankle-turning, stony track to reach Devil's Chair, about which there are many legends.
- Continue on same path past Devil's Chair to reach intersection of paths before next rocky outcrop, where go right, descending gradually to gate with Shropshire Way sign.
- Go through gate at edge of Stiperstones National Nature Reserve and follow track diagonally downhill to two fingerposts at junction of paths.
- At second fingerpost go left through The Hollies farm on stony track till reaching surfaced lane, where go right.
- Follow lane downhill for one mile to Stedment, where join lane coming in from right and follow down to junction with road, where go left and then immediately right at next junction to reach Horseshoe Inn at Bridges.

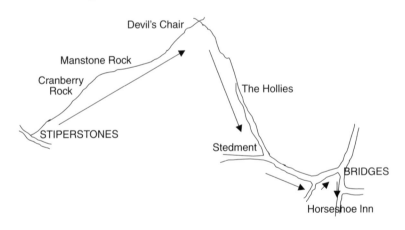

THE DEVIL'S CHAIR

The Devil's Chair got its name from a time when the Devil came from Ireland with a leather apron full of stones either to block Hell Gutter on the other side of the hill or to dam the River Severn. He sat down to rest but, when he rose, his apron strings broke and the stones were scattered all around. The Devil still visits here, sitting on his chair in the belief that by doing so he will push the Stiperstones under the ground so that England, which he hates, will perish.

Stipertones has captured the imagination of writers and painters, of

whom the most famous is D.H. Lawrence, who used the Devil's Chair as part of the setting in his novel "St Mawr". But it

The Devil's Chair

is Shropshire's own novelist, Mary Webb, who was most intrigued by Stiperstones, knowing the area well. She renamed the ridge as the Diafol Mountains and described the Devil's Chair as "like a fist flourished in the face" in her novel "The Golden Arrow".

BRIDGES

You can barely call this a hamlet but it once was an important crossing point with its two bridges, one for those on foot over the stony River West Onny and one for vehicles over the Darnford Brook. The isolated Horseshoe Inn (Tel: 01588-650260), open all day every day from 12 except Monday, is a splendid place for refuelling with its log fire, its strange windows, and its friendly pub cat. It also serves excellent Real Ales, usually Adnams, Timothy Taylor Landlord and Shepherd Neame, plus extremely good lunches. Also offers accommodation.

Stamping point at bar or, when closed, on outside wall.

Horseshoe Inn

Bridges to Church Stretton (5 miles)

- Take narrow road, signed Adstone Walk, from Horseshoe Inn at Bridges climbing past Onny Bank Farm but, when Shropshire Way/Adstone Walk goes to right, keep climbing on road to reach Coates Farm.
- Go through farm buildings and, ignoring sign to Medlicott, go left past farmhouse on to rising Jack Mytton Way.
- Follow track through several gates for almost two miles as it winds up to top of Long Mynd.
- On reaching road, go right and after 20 yards go left through car parking space and past tumulus on The Portway (ancient track across the Long Mynd used by sheep drovers).
- When other wide track joins in from right, go left till reaching wooden post with *"Carding Mill"* on it on right.
- Go right and immediately right again on to stone-covered path descending into Carding Mill Valley.
- On reaching junction of streams and paths, keep straight ahead to reach Chalet Pavilion tearooms and National Trust shop (open Easter to end of October from 11–5 for very good cakes, etc.) in Carding Mill Valley.
- After refreshments, take Carding Mill Valley road to junction with B4370 then go right into Church Stretton.

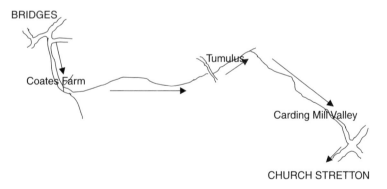

THE LONG MYND

The Long Mynd, literally "The Long Mountain", stretches almost fifteen miles and is a prominent feature in the area. Much of it is now in the care of the National Trust and its slopes are magnets for hundreds of picnickers, walkers and, in season, for whinberry-pickers. Whinberry-picking used to be a major and important activity for the people of the Long Mynd villages, as this account reveals:

> To the poor people for miles around the whinberry picking is the great event of the year. The whole family betakes themselves to the hill with the early morning carrying with them the provisions for the day; and not infrequently a kettle to prepare tea forms part of their heavy load. I know no more picturesque sight than that presented by the summit of the Long Mynd towards four o'clock on an August afternoon when the numerous fires are lit among the heather and as many kettles steaming away on top of them, while noisy chattering groups of women and children are clustered around, glad to rest after a hard day's work.

Once picked, the whinberries were laden into huge baskets and taken to Shrewsbury market.

The Midland Gliding Club that operates from the flat top of the Long Mynd has been in existence since 1930 and once included the well-known flier Amy Johnson among its members.

CARDING MILL VALLEY

Once a major thoroughfare for sheep and thus a place for wool-carding, Carding Mill Valley has long been a favourite place for family picnics, for children damming streams, and for those starting walks over the Long Mynd. Pause a while at the National Trust tearooms for refreshment and contemplation.

Carding Mill Valley

CHURCH STRETTON PIX

Sheila-na-gig, St Lawrence's Church

Hesba Stratton's Million Seller

Church Stretton Market

Stretton Hills Water

Buck's Head

Long Mynd Hotel

CHURCH STRETTON STORY

The name Stretton is Saxon, indicating a farm by a paved road, and that road was the one, known as Watling Street, that the Romans drove through the Stretton Gap between their forts at Leintwardine and Wroxeter. The earliest mention of the town is in the Domesday Book of 1086 when it was held by Earl Edwin of Shrewsbury and was worth 100 shillings. The original Saxon church of St Lawrence (who was burned to death by the Emperor Valerian on a gridiron, though not one made by George Foreman) was rebuilt by the Normans in the 12th century.

Church Stretton became a market town in 1214, thanks to a charter from King John, and there is evidence of its growing importance as a "route town" from tolls collected during the following century. That status grew as the herds of sheep were driven across the Long Mynd into Church Stretton's market, often down the deadly Burway, the hairpin-bending road that leads over the hills and which has been the cause of many an accident. The November Fair held in Church Stretton was known as Deadman's Fair because of the number of people who died on the hills on their way home, having enjoyed the local Real Ales too much.

However, it was in Victorian times that the town really began to prosper as it became a fashionable place for ladies and gentlemen of a certain social caste to come for the fresh air and fine views of the Shropshire hills. In 1912 the official handbook of the Church Stretton Advancement Association described it thus:

> *"Not only has the climate a generally tonic and invigorating effect, but it also has the valuable quality of exercising a somewhat tranquillising influence on the nervous system and circulation."*

Better than valium anyway!

The opening of the Hydropathic Establishment (now the upmarket Long Mynd Hotel) in 1901 cemented this reputation, although its health-giving waters had to be brought by train from Llandrindod Wells. There are natural springs, however, that provide Stretton Hills Water, which is marketed all over the world but which locals and visitors can get free from a tap outside the bottling plant just out of town.

In the latter half of the 20th century, Church Stretton's peacefulness drew large numbers of retired people to settle there but in recent years the town has sought to attract a wider range of visitors, marketing itself as *"Little Switzerland"*.

CHURCH STRETTON CELEBRITIES

SHEILA-NA-GIG

The Sheila-na-gig is a figure from medieval stone carvings of a grinning woman holding open her vulva. This particular Sheila can be found above the blocked-up Norman door on the outside of St Lawrence's Church.

Sheila-na-gigs are seen by some to be medieval allegories of lust; others see them as magical figures that cured infertility in women; others believe they are an echo of the ancient Earth Mother.

The curious thing is that such rather rude-looking figures are generally found in the décor of churches, suggesting either that the ministers of these churches were dirty old men or, more likely, that the Christian churches embraced some of the pagan symbols in order to convince folk that Christianity was just as much fun as their primitive beliefs.

REV. DONALD CARR

The Rev. Donald Carr was a minister of St Michael's Church in the tiny village of Woolstaston on the Long Mynd who, every Sunday for eight and a half years, had walked across the Mynd to the church in Ratlinghope to conduct the service there.

On 29th January 1865, Rev. Carr set out on his regular journey, though he was travelling in heavy snow. Because of the snowdrifts on the hills, Carr frequently had to crawl on his hands and knees, till he reached Ratlinghope, conducted the service and set off home.

The weather had become worse by now, with fierce winds and a heavy storm. In the whitened landscape and with darkness encroaching, Carr was forced off his accustomed path and found himself sliding down ravines, losing his boots and becoming snow-blind. Eventually, as morning broke, he heard children's voices and was rescued. He arrived back in Church Stretton at 2 pm, exactly 22 hours after he had set out.

HESBA STRETTON (1832–1911)

Hesba Stratton, who was really Sarah Smith from Wellington, was a very popular children's author of Victorian times. Hesba Stretton's stories are all very moral pieces, deeply sentimental but very much in tune with the times. Her best-known book was *Jessica's First Prayer*, which sold a million and a half copies – astonishing! She was ashamed of the poverty of so many young children in those days and helped to found what later became the NSPCC.

Although she never lived in Church Stretton, there is a memorial window to Hesba Stretton in St Lawrence's Church.

CHURCH STRETTON CAKES

BERRY'S COFFEE HOUSE, High Street
Berry's offers light lunches, clotted cream teas, home-made scones and cakes and Shropshire ice cream in Queen Anne house with courtyard. Food is sourced locally and organic if possible. Shropshire tea/coffee shop of the year in 2004.

CHALET PAVILION TEAROOMS, Carding Mill Valley
Fresh coffee, cream teas, home-made cakes, etc., near the end of your day's journey.

HOLLYBUSH CAFÉ, Burway Road
Snacks, sandwiches, tea/coffee, home-made cakes plus a lovely warm welcome. Popular with walkers because open on Sundays through the year.

VICTORIA HOUSE TEAROOM, High Street
Fascinating Victorian shop with tearooms serving home-made cakes, tea and coffee. All products sourced locally and organic if possible. Only open at weekends.

CHURCH STRETTON ALE

BUCK'S HEAD HOTEL, High Street
Serves excellent selection of Real Ales – Hobsons, Timothy Taylor Landlord, Greene King IPA, Old Bucks and Worthington Cask Bitter, plus good pub grub. Situated near the roundabout in the middle of town. Beer garden at the back.

KING'S ARMS, High Street
Small old-fashioned pub that serves a changing selection of Real Ales. Open all day on Sunday.

WINE VAULTS, High Street
One of the narrowest pubs in Shropshire. Bar snacks and coffee served. Pool table. Serious dominoes pub. Handy for the chippy next door. Serves a changing selection of Real Ales.

OLD COPPERS MALT HOUSE, Shrewsbury Road
Good food menu and open all day on Sundays. Pool table and darts in the bar. Jukebox has a very good selection of 70's rock. Serves Charles Wells Bombardier and Greene King Abbot Ale.

CHURCH STRETTON ACCOMMODATION

BELVEDERE GUEST HOUSE, Burway Road, Church Stretton, SY6 6DP
(Tel: 01694-722322)

BROOKFIELDS GUEST HOUSE, Watling Street North,
Church Stretton, SY6 7AR (Tel: 01694-722314)

OLD RECTORY HOUSE, Burway Road, Church Stretton, SY6 6DW
(Tel: 01694-724462)

RHEINGOLD, 9 The Bridleways, Church Stretton, SY6 7AN
(Tel: 01694-723969)

HIGHCLIFFE, Madeira Walk, Church Stretton, SY6 6JQ
(Tel: 01694-722908)

BEECHCROFT GUEST HOUSE, 32 Shrewsbury Road, Church Stretton,
SY6 6JB (Tel: 01694-722929)

VINE COTTAGE, 81 Shrewsbury Road, Church Stretton, SY6 6EY
(Tel: 01694-723947)

OAKBANK, Cunnery Road, Church Stretton, SY6 6AQ
(Tel: 01694-720181)

VICTORIA HOUSE, 48 High St, Church Stretton, SY6 6BX
(Tel: 01694-723823)

CHURCH STRETTON SERVICES

Post Office: in the Spar supermarket

Banks with ATM: Lloyds and Barclays in High Street, HSBC in Burway,
Co-op in Easthope Road

Visitor Information Centre: Church Street (Tel: 01694-723133)

Transport connections: mainline railway station with regular
connections to Shrewsbury.

CHURCH STRETTON – MUCH WENLOCK

OS Map: Explorer 217

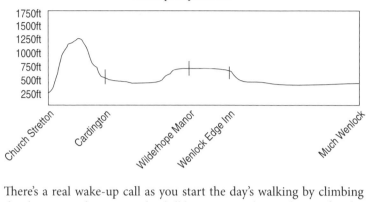

There's a real wake-up call as you start the day's walking by climbing the sharp rise of Caer Caradoc hill but, once you've made your height, there's a lovely ridge walk to its highest point for dramatic views before you descend to the ancient village of Cardington. Then there's a cross-country amble to reach the long wooded limestone escarpment of Wenlock Edge and head towards the splendid Elizabethan Wilderhope Manor, now in the care of the National Trust and operating as a Youth Hostel.

After passing Wilderhope Manor, you maintain your height on Wenlock Edge till reaching the tiny village of Easthope and shortly afterwards arrive at the atmospheric Wenlock Edge Inn for mid-walk refreshments. Then it's downhill into the Wenlock woodlands again to visit Ippikin's Rock and to pass by Major's Leap on the old railway line that is now the Jack Mytton Way for riders and the Shropshire Way for walkers.

Finally you emerge from the woodland on the outskirts of the lovely old town of Much Wenlock, with its ancient Priory ruins and its interesting claim to be the originator of the modern Olympic Games movement.

PLACE	DAILY MILES	TOTAL MILES
Church Stretton	–	76.5
Cardington	4	80.5
Wilderhope Manor	8	84.5
Wenlock Edge Inn	11	87.5
Much Wenlock	15	91.5

CHURCH STRETTON – MUCH WENLOCK
(15 miles)

Church Stretton to Cardington (4 miles)

- Leave Church Stretton by going down Sandford Avenue towards the A49 and by Fire Station go left into Essex Road then right at next junction and follow road till Public Footpath sign, taking you through gardens of Old People's Home.
- Take path to stile and cross railway lines very carefully (keep your eyes and ears peeled!) to further stile and path alongside BMX park up to stile on to A49 road.
- Cross main road to further footpath sign, over a small field, another stile, a track (this was the original Watling Street – imagine those Legions marching past), another stile then go diagonally left across field to final stile on to surfaced road.
- Go left on road till gates leading to New House Farm but go right, following fingerpost for Caer Caradoc, skirting field up to further gate and stile leading to clear track past fish ponds.
- After 50 yards, look for narrow path on left leading to footbridge over stream, then shortly afterwards take steeply-ascending footpath on left up Caer Caradoc, past Three Fingers Rock and follow terrific ridge walk to summit.

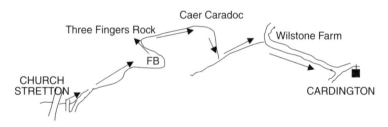

- At highest point, go 90° right to gap in fort and take steep downhill path to gate and clear track across field to path (yes, the one you left to climb Caer Caradoc!).
- Go left on track and follow to junction with road at Wilstone Farm, where go right and follow road for approximately one mile to footbridge by ford and road junction.
- Go left past magnificent Brook House into Cardington and then right by churchyard of St James's Church (enter to see a remarkable effigy!).

CAER CARADOC

Caer Caradoc is only 900 feet high but, rising sharply as it does from the valley bottom, it feels much higher. It gives breathtaking views of the Shropshire hills.

Caer Caradoc Ridge from Three Fingers Rock

The oval hill-fort of the Cornovii tribe on its summit is clearly defined, with its inner and outer banks and southern gateway.

Caer Caradoc was allegedly where Caractacus made his final stand against the Roman army.

CARDINGTON

Cardington is a very ancient village, as many of its stone buildings suggest. At the time of the Domesday Book in 1086 it was held by Reginald the Sheriff and was later given to the Knights Templar.

The Royal Oak is believed to be the oldest pub in Shropshire. It's a lovely old pub with a welcoming fireplace, serving food every day except Monday from 12 to 2 pm and Hobsons, Shropshire Lad and Old Speckled Hen Real Ales (Tel 01694-771266).

The unusual effigy inside St James's Church of a man lying in a very uncomfortable position commemorates Chief Justice Leighton who lived nearby at Plaish Hall. The Judge persuaded a local bricklayer he was about to imprison to build him the finest chimneys in the country, in return for which he would be set free. The bricklayer laboured for months to create the most remarkable chimneys, for which the Judge repaid him by hanging him from one of them.

The inscription on Judge Leighton's memorial reads: Nemo ante obitum beatus (No one is happy before death). Miserable old sod!!

Chief Justice Leighton

Cardington to Wilderhope Manor (4 miles)

- Just past St James's Church and on opposite side of road, look for narrow footpath between two cottages, leading to three metal kissing gates and footbridge over stream.
- At stile go straight ahead, following right side of four fields, each with stiles and gates, and 20 yards after fourth gate look for stile to bridleway sign in tree-lined route to right (may be fenced in).
- Take bridleway for 50 yards and look for hidden stile in trees to left, then follow field downhill on left to stile and footbridge over stream, then stile into field.
- Climb briefly up field to gate in left corner and on to road by Stone House, where go right for 30 yards and left at first gate. Immediately go left through next gate and follow hedge on right side of field to metal gate.
- Maintain line across field to corner of hedge and follow right side of field through three gates as path becomes bridleway, then two further gates to road where go left into East Wall. Follow road through East Wall bending right to reach B4371 and go straight across on road signposted Wenlock Edge Farm (or, if running late, go left for half mile to Longville Arms 01694-771206).
- Follow surfaced road past Milton Cottage and just before next new house on right, look for footpath sign to right leading into field and footpath diagonally left across field.
- Go straight ahead on clear path through two fields to deep hedge and stile, then path across further field to stile into wood, where take path ascending diagonally to right and after 50 yards look for stepped path on left rising sharply to top of Coats Wood on Wenlock Edge.
- At junction of path with broader Jack Mytton Way, go left and follow bridleway to cross road and down surfaced track till reaching Wilderhope Manor.

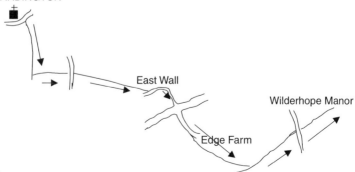

WILDERHOPE MANOR

Wilderhope Manor was built around 1586 for Francis and Ellen Smallman who lived there until 1599.

It is a magnificent Elizabethan building with solid limestone walls, wonderful long chimney stacks (how Justice Leighton would have envied them), mullioned windows, plaster ceilings and a superb spiral wooden staircase.

Wilderhope Manor is now in the care of the National Trust, but open to visitors once or twice a week. (Tel: 08707-706090 for opening hours). It also operates as a Youth Hostel and a brilliantly atmospheric place it is.

Mary Webb called it Undern Hall in her novel "Precious Bane" and described it thus:

> "Undern Hall, with its many small-paned windows, faced the north sullenly. It was a place of which the influence and magic were not good. Even in May, when the lilacs frothed into purple, paved the lawn with shadows, steeped the air with scent;…still, something that haunted the place set the heart fluttering. No place is its own, and that which is most stained with old tumults has the strongest fascination."

Wilderhope Manor

Wilderhope Manor to Wenlock Edge Inn (3 miles)

- Take track going left behind Wilderhope Manor (waymarked Shropshire Way) and follow this until junction with road, where go right towards Pilgrim Cottage.
- Go left immediately past Pilgrim Cottage and follow path by hedge, becoming wider track as it approaches Lutwyche Hall glimpsed on the left.
- Just past Lutwyche Hall, after going through gates by Hall Farm which appears to specialise in manure, look for stile on right into field and follow left side of field up to gate.
- Take track over stile past house on right and on to road.
- Go right into tiny hamlet of Easthope and visit the churchyard for some interesting tales.

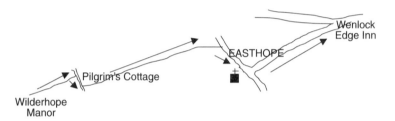

- At road junction by Manor Farm, go left on road signposted Much Wenlock and climb gradually, passing kangaroo warning sign, to join B4371.
- At road junction, go right to Wenlock Edge Inn.

WENLOCK EDGE INN

The Wenlock Edge Inn (Tel:01746-785678) is a smashing little pub that serves great food and Hobsons beers. It's also the home of a Storytelling Club that meets here every month. However, it's only open at lunchtimes 12 – 2 pm from Wednesday to Sunday.

Stamping point at bar or, when closed, on outside wall.

Wenlock Edge Inn

PILGRIM COTTAGE

Pilgrim Cottage is believed to be named after Richard More, who with his three siblings was sent on *The Mayflower* in 1620 because their father, of nearby Larden Hall, had discovered that a certain Jacob Blakeway and not he was the true begetter of the four children. Three of the children died on the voyage but Richard More survived and was thus one of the original Pilgrim Fathers who founded America.

Pilgrim Cottage

LUTWYCHE HALL

Lutwyche Hall was the birthplace of Stella Benson [1892–1933], a now-forgotten feminist writer who was friendly with such more notable writers as Victoria Sackville-West and Winifred Holtby. Never heard of her? Me neither.

EASTHOPE

In St Peter's churchyard are two tombs, bearing no marking but a simple cross. Here lie two monks, former residents of Manor Farm, originally a cell of Wenlock Priory, who one night began a fierce argument. They came to blows, struggled together, fell down the cellar steps and were killed. Their ghosts are still arguing.

In 1333 the Vicar of St Peter's, Will Garmston, killed the church's patron, John de Easthope, and the Vicar's ghost still haunts the churchyard.

Nice people, those Christians, eh?

St Peter's Church and Churchyard

Wenlock Edge Inn to Much Wenlock (4 miles)

- Cross road opposite Wenlock Edge Inn and take permissive path across car park then through three gates to find Ippikin's Rock.
- If you've survived Ippikin, go right again on descending stepped path, then, on joining wider track go left to find old railway track. Go right and continue for some time till reaching bridleway gate on left opposite track coming in from right.
- Go left through gate and descend to road, where cross to clear farm track till reaching gate on right signposted Jack Mytton Way, where go through and ascend on middle of three paths.
- Where track levels out, join Shropshire Way coming in from right from Presthope and continue. Where there is a fork, ignore Blakeway Farm sign and keep right.
- At clearing, ignore sign to Blakeway Farm and continue on track signposted Much Wenlock, noting views of The Wrekin on left and passing stepped path to Major's Leap on right.
- Where track through woodland on Wenlock Edge ends, go through gate and go straight ahead on hedge-rimmed lane descending gradually into Blakeway Hollow, where further gate leads to surfaced road and B4371.
- Go left at B4371 and, at junction with A458, cross road and go right on raised walkway and follow into centre of Much Wenlock.

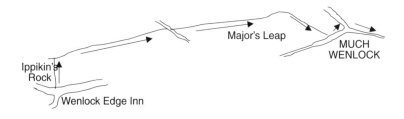

IPPIKIN'S ROCK

Anyone who stands on this rock and has the nerve to shout:

"Ippikin, Ippikin,
Keep away with your long chin"

will see the robber's ghost but run the risk of being pushed over to their death.

Ippikin and his bandits terrorised the locality. No-one dared approach his cave for fear of attack, even though it was rumoured to be full of treasure. The robber had his come-uppance when lightning

Ippikin's Rock

struck a huge rock overhanging the cave. It toppled, crashing down across the entrance and trapping Ippikin and his murderous band inside.

MAJOR'S LEAP

Major's Leap commemorates Thomas Smallman, the owner of Wilderhope Manor during the Civil War, who was a major in the Royalist Army captured by Cromwell's troops while carrying despatches from Bridgnorth

to Shrewsbury. He was imprisoned at Wilderhope Manor but escaped, probably by means of an old garderobe flue, and fled on his horse.

The fierceness of his captors' pursuit forced Smallman off the road and over Wenlock Edge. Although his horse was killed, a crab-apple tree broke the Major's fall. His pursuers assumed that he was dead but, once they had left, Smallman climbed up the hill and continued to Shrewsbury. Or so they say!

Major's Leap

MUCH WENLOCK PIX

Guildhall

William Penny Brookes Plaque

Raynald's Mansion

George and Dragon

St Milburga's Well

Wenlock Abbey

MUCH WENLOCK STORY

*"An ancient little town at the Abbey gates.... a town indeed with
no great din of vehicles, but with goodly brick houses, with a
dozen publics (public houses), with tidy whitewashed cottages
and with little girls bobbing curtsies in the street."*

Henry James

Wenlock's origins lie in the ruins of the 7th century Wenlock Priory,
founded by the son of Penda, King of the Mercians, whose grand-
daughter Milburga was its first abbess (by the by, her father was NOT
called Cheeseburga). The abbey was destroyed and rebuilt at least once
before the Norman conquest but it was substantially remodelled by
Roger de Montgomery in the 11th century and was the major reason
for the town's existence until its dissolution in 1540. The Priory,
looked after now by English Heritage, is well worth a visit to see some
fascinating and beautiful architectural structures.

The town itself began to develop in the 12th century with the
remodelling of the Holy Trinity parish church, in whose grounds, by
a stroke of remarkable good fortune, were discovered the bones of
Milburga in 1101. The bones were placed in a shrine, a top bishop
was summoned and, when the bishop's wife was cured of a mysterious
disease by drinking water in which the bones had been washed, St
Milburga's shrine became a site for pilgrims seeking miracle cures, and
Much Wenlock began to prosper.

Next to the church is the Guildhall, built by a local carpenter in 1540,
to provide a covered area for the town market, for which purpose it
is still used. Later the Guildhall came to incorporate the magistrates'
court, the prison and the punishment stocks, though sadly the latter are
no longer available for the local happy slappers.

Apart from being the site of pilgrimages, Much Wenlock's wealth
has been created from the agricultural lands that surround it and from
the limestone quarrying that still occurs on Wenlock Edge. The ridge
known as Wenlock Edge is one of the most famous geological sites in
the world, because it comprises limestone that was originally formed
from crushed shells, salt water and ancient, tiny sea creatures in the
Silurian period some 425 million years ago. The Edge abounds, as you
will have noticed, with fossils.

Nowadays, Much Wenlock acts as a commuter town for Shrewsbury
and the West Midlands conurbation, as well as a safe retirement area. Its
old streets, its many attractive and varied buildings, its historic edifices,
together with its independent shops, make it an attraction for those
modern-day pilgrims, the tourists.

MUCH WENLOCK CELEBRITIES

St Milburga (?–715)

Milburga was the daughter of Merewald of the royal Mercian household. She was appointed abbess of the priory at Much Wenlock in 690 A.D. and was renowned for her ability to cure the sick, to communicate with birds, and to charm scarecrows (very useful!). She had been promised in marriage to Wolfgang, a Saxon lord, but turned him down because of her religious vows even though she still had the hots for him. Milburga died in 715, already a saint. Her well still allegedly cures eye diseases and scrofula, but sadly (for Cakes and Ale walkers) not blisters.

William Penny Brookes (1809–1895)

William Penny Brookes is, with considerable justification, considered to be the true founder of the modern Olympic Games. Dr. Brookes, a Wenlock native, was a noted benefactor who instituted the Wenlock Olympian Games for the moral and physical improvement of the local workers, though what moral value there was in pig-chasing or blindfold wheelbarrow-pushing is hard to fathom. Brookes was famously visited in 1890 by Baron de Coubertin, who of course six years later started the modern Olympic Games movement and claimed the idea as his own. Typical French perfidy.

Mary Webb (1881–1927)

Mary Webb, the Shropshire novelist, lived her early life in The Grange on the outskirts of Much Wenlock. She developed a deep love of the Shropshire countryside and its folklore and used these in her novels. The best known of these are *Gone to Earth* and *Precious Bane*, both of which were made into films, the latter in Much Wenlock itself using local people as extras. Although her work was much admired in its day, modern readers might find it a bit twee. Well, I do!

Nanny Morgan (?–1857)

Nanny Morgan was a witch employed by her neighbours to ill-wish those against whom they had a grudge. She was murdered by her lodger, a man called Wright, who killed her to escape from her spiritual thralldom. After her death, letters were found in her cottage, consulting her on various matters, written in the Devil's tongue. They were all burnt by order of the Mayor in the yard of The Talbot Inn before all the townsfolk of Much Wenlock. Shame!

MUCH WENLOCK CAKES

CAROL ANNE'S TEAROOMS/RESTAURANT, Wilmore Street
Comfortably furnished tearooms offering a range of sandwiches and afternoon teas.

COPPER KETTLE, High Street
Bijou tearooms right in the heart of the town, serving tasty cakes and snacks.

THE DELI, High Street
If you can get past the delicious offerings of the delicatessen, the café at the back offers welcoming teas, coffees, cakes and pastries.

MUCH WENLOCK ALE

GASKELL ARMS
Hotel on the main road through Much Wenlock. Food served. Small homely bar and lounge. Restaurant area. Bar has a cast iron stove and a collection of water jugs. Serves Courage Directors and Theakstons Best.

GEORGE & DRAGON
Traditional pub with very friendly feel. Low ceilings, beams and a huge collection of water jugs. Food served but not Sunday or Wednesday evenings. Excellent selection of Real Ales, including Abbot, Greene King IPA, Hobsons, Smiles Heritage, Timothy Taylor Landlord. Quiz night every other week.

RAVEN HOTEL
Three star hotel with a small comfortable bar that serves Bass and Wood's Shropshire Lad. Food served and friendly service.

TALBOT INN
Very popular with diners because this is a comfortable, traditional old pub with plenty of beams. Serves Bass and Youngs. Excellent food served, though not cheap.

MUCH WENLOCK ACCOMMODATION

RAVEN HOTEL, Barrow Street, Much Wenlock, TF13 6EN
(Tel: 01952-727251)

GASKELL ARMS HOTEL, Shrewsbury Road, Much Wenlock,
TF13 6AQ (Tel: 01952-727212)

TALBOT INN, High Street, Much Wenlock, TF13 6AA
(Tel: 01952-727077)

BASTARD HALL, 57 Shineton Street, Much Wenlock
(Tel: 01952-728775)

WENLOCK POTTERY B&B, Shineton Street, Much Wenlock,
TF13 6HT (Tel: 01952-727600)

DANYWENALLT, Farley Road, Much Wenlock, TF13 6NB
(Tel: 01952-727892)

CARNEWYDD, Farley Road, Much Wenlock, TF13 6NB
(Tel: 01952-728417)

MUCH WENLOCK SERVICES

Post Office: High Street

Banks with ATM: HSBC on High Street and petrol station on
Shrewsbury-Bridgnorth road

Visitor Information Centre (seasonal): The Museum, High Street
(Tel: 01952-727679)

Transport connections: regular bus service 436 to Shrewsbury, where
there is a mainline railway station.

MUCH WENLOCK – BRIDGNORTH

OS Map: Explorer 242 & 218

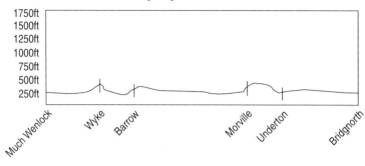

This is a steady day's walking, following the route of the Shropshire Way out of Much Wenlock past Wenlock Priory eventually climbing slightly to the little hamlet of Wyke, where there are good views of the Long Mynd and the Clee Hills. Then you pick up the Jack Mytton Way to take you on a slightly raised route to Barrow and its attractive church, where a legendary whipper-in is buried.

The next stage of the journey is indeed a journey through history. Initially you walk on Jack Mytton Way then around the edge of the Willey estate. Then, branching off the Jack Mytton Way, your route takes you through the grounds and past the magnificent 1691 Hall of Aldenham Park, with its long associations with the Acton family, and into the village of Morville. The Acton Arms is an appropriate mid-journey refreshment point.

The final stage of the day's journey takes you on a sharp but brief ascent through woodland to Meadowley then on pleasant cross-country paths through the tiny hamlet of Underton and finally into Bridgnorth by the station for the Severn Valley Railway, whose Railwayman's Arms provides a suitable site for end-of-journey celebrations.

PLACE	DAILY MILES	TOTAL MILES
Much Wenlock	–	91.5
Wyke	2.5	94
Barrow	5	96.5
Morville	10	101.5
Underton	12	103.5
Bridgnorth	14.5	106

MUCH WENLOCK – BRIDGNORTH
(14.5 miles)

Much Wenlock to Barrow (5 miles)

- Leave Much Wenlock by going left in front of the Guildhall, past Holy Trinity Church, then right past Wenlock Priory on surfaced lane around edge of Willey estate, bending to right and gate to Downs Mill (note Shropshire Way sign).
- Continue on track to right of Downs Mill cottages, emerging at stile and footbridge over brook, then go left on clear track across field to stile and continue to Bradley Farm.
- Cross minor road at Bradley Farm to go left between farm buildings to stile on right, followed by further stile to left and after stiles go diagonally left across large field to stile in opposite corner (aim for Ironbridge Power Station).
- Follow hedge on right of next field to gate on right half-way down field, where go through and over stile into field and follow path straight across past large oak tree and down to stile in bottom corner of field in front of farmhouse.
- Over stile follow track past Woodhouse Farm going right through woodland till reaching surfaced lane, where go right through Acklands Coppice and, as woodland thins, notice Tickwood Hall and Audience Meadow on left.

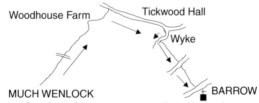

- Keep on surfaced road as it rises to reach Wyke and at road junction, go right downhill till reaching fingerpost for Jack Mytton Way on left.
- Go through woodland and keep to left of fields with gates and, after second gate, keep to left-hand hedge for 50 yards till break in hedge. Go left uphill to hedge.
- Go right along side of hedge, passing medieval Cultivation Terraces of now disappeared Arlescott Village settlement, till reaching gate and farm track, where go straight ahead to road.
- Cross road, still on Jack Mytton Way, and take raised path across middle of field till reaching road at Barrow opposite St Giles' Church and Tom Moody's grave.

AUDIENCE MEADOW

Audience Meadow is where in 1642 Charles 1 met the local squirearchy to ask for financial support.

Tickwood Hall was, until a few years ago, the home of Lady Dugdale, one of the Queen's longest-serving Ladies-in-Waiting.

Tickwood Hall with Audience Meadow

Lady Dugdale, once described on a state visit to the Vatican as "a stately galleon in full sail," introduced medicinal alcohol into the Ladies-in-Waiting's sitting room at the Palace. Now there's fame.

TOM MOODY 1756–1796

St. Giles Church, Barrow

Tom Moody, who worked for Lord Forester of Willey, was regarded as the best whipper-in in the whole of England.

Travellers would frequently leave their coaches to listen to his tales of the hunt and his songs at The Hangman's Gate inn.

His dying wish was to be buried under a yew tree in Barrow churchyard, his coffin having been borne by six earth-stoppers, followed by his horse carrying all his hunting paraphernalia together with four of his old hounds, and for three view-halloos to be shouted over his grave.

You all knew Tom Moody, the whipper-in, well.
The bell just done tolling was honest Tom's knell,
A more able sportsman ne'er follow'd a hound,
Thro' a country well known to him fifty miles round.
No hound ever open'd with Tom near the wood,
But he'd challenge the tone and could tell if t'was good,
And all with attention, would eagerly mark,
When he cheer'd up the pack, – "Hark!
To Rockwood, hark! hark!
High! wind him! and cross him!
Now, Ratler, boy, bark."

87

Barrow to Morville (5 miles)

- Take surfaced track past church to Barrow House, where go straight ahead over two stiles and continue on Jack Mytton Way through copse. At end of copse, go through two gates and then past trees to further gate.
- Go diagonally left across next field (or round left field boundaries) towards gap in hedge and post. Follow bridleway with hedge on right up to road. Go left on road to reach road junction where go left again past Shirlett Farm on edge of Willey estate.
- Follow lane (possibly longest cul-de-sac in UK) for approximately one mile till reaching road end at Firs Farm, where go straight ahead on delightful tree-lined grass track leading over and down Round Hill.
- At end of woodland, keep straight ahead to reach road and go right till reaching sign for Hurst Farm Lakes.
- Go right and follow rising track to Hurst Farm, keeping straight on between lakes (beware model aircraft coming in from right), then rising to junction of paths at top of hill, where go left.
- Follow main track, ignoring all left turns, till emerging in front of magnificent Aldenham Park, family seat of the Lords Acton, and take wonderful long tree-lined avenue down through splendid wrought-iron gates.
- Passing through the gates (pausing only to consider Lord Acton's words as you note the PRIVATE sign) cross busy main road and look for stile in left corner of hedge.
- Follow left hedge through two fields to steps and stile on to minor road, where go left and at road junction (notice old Whipping Post) go right into Morville for Acton Arms.

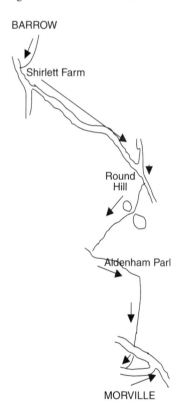

BARROW

Shirlett Farm

Round Hill

Aldenham Park

MORVILLE

WILLEY

The Willey estate has been the property of the Forester family since 1748, though the classical-style Willey Hall was only built in 1812.

Willey New Furnace on the estate was where Jack "Iron-Mad" Wilkinson, who had come from Cumbria to work with Abraham Darby at Coalbrookdale, invented a device for precision boring of cylinders which was crucial in enabling Matthew Boulton and James Watt to develop the steam engine.

Willey New Furnace was also where Wilkinson built The Trial, the first iron barge to be used on the River Severn, which, when launched in 1787, disappointed a huge crowd who had turned up expecting it to sink.

ALDENHAM PARK

Lord Acton (1834-1902), the historian and adviser to Gladstone, lived at Aldenham Park. He it was who wrote the immortal and often misquoted statement: "Power tends to corrupt and absolute power corrupts absolutely."

Lord Acton's Aldenham library of 60,000 books was purchased on his death by the American entrepreneur Andrew Carnegie, through whom they were later donated to Cambridge University.

Lady Daphne Acton (1912-2003) was a leading Roman Catholic and gave Monsignor Ronald Knox a home at Aldenham so that he could complete his translation of the bible while acting as the family chaplain. His peaceful retreat was threatened at the outbreak of World War II when 55 convent girls were evacuated from London to live there.

The wrought-iron gates to the hall come from the 1851 Great Exhibition at Crystal Palace. According to legend, the replica of an armoured leg dripping blood displayed above the gates commemorates an early Acton who cut off his own leg and threw it across the stream to claim ownership of the land on which it fell.

Aldenham Park

Morville to Bridgnorth (4.5 miles)

- Retrace steps to take signed path up drive to Morville Hall and St Gregory's Church.
- Go left behind church and, in line with church tower, find footbridge over Mor Brook, then climb diagonally left across fields to metal gate into woodland.
- Through gate take indistinct and twisting path through woods heading broadly left (look for blue tape markers on trees).
- Go through gate at end of woodland and follow left hand side of field to gate. Go left and follow hedge to two successive gates on to farm track leading through farm buildings into Meadowley.
- Cross road on to bridleway (signposted Jack Mytton Way) and after 100 yards at bridleway sign go through gate on left and, where hedge bends left, aim for isolated oak tree and follow bridleway across two fields, to reach gate by top corner of Underton Plantation.
- Follow diagonally left line to further gate, then though hedge towards West Farm, where take bridleway signs to right of farm buildings and on to road.

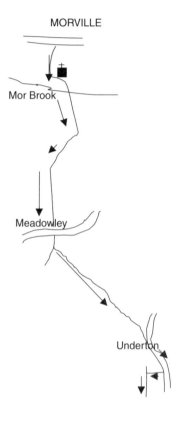

- Follow road through Underton for short distance past a PO box and friendly sign for The Barn and past East Farm to footpath sign to right through orchard with two gates on to green track.
- Take green lane to left then follow footpath signs right and then left to pass by right side of two pools, keeping close to pools.

MORVILLE

The Norman church of St Gregory, replacing an earlier Saxon church on the same site, was consecrated in 1118 when two women and five horses were killed by lightning as they left the ceremony.

Entrance to St Gregory's Church

Morville Hall was built in 1546, replacing and using the stones of Morville Priory – it was altered into its present Georgian style in 1750s. It passed into the hands of the Acton family in the 19th century.

The Dower House Gardens within the grounds of the hall have a sequence of separate gardens designed in the style of different historical periods, including a Turf Maze and an Elizabethan Knot Garden. They were designed by Dr Katherine Swift, gardening columnist for The Times.

Fancy a laugh? Look out for the ha-ha that separates the path from the gardens of the hall.

THE ACTON ARMS

The Acton Arms was originally the Abbot's lodging for Morville Priory. It is allegedly haunted by the ghost of Richard Marshall, the 28th Abbot of Shrewsbury, who lived there until the dissolution of the monasteries in 1540.

Acton Arms

The Acton Arms is open every day, selling excellent Banks's beers, and food from 12 to 3 pm Mon-Fri and all day Sat/Sun (Tel: 01746-714209).

Stamping point at bar or, when closed, on wall by rear door.

- Past two pools look for stile in hedge ahead and cross field to gate, where go left on road for 100 yards, ignoring road to Underton to road junction by Harpsford Mill Farm.
- Opposite Harpswood Bridge go through gate and follow footpath to top of rise and down to gate by road.
- Follow road for half mile to stile on left at bend in road.
- Over stile, keep to left side of field to further stile into lane, where go left.
- Follow lane to footbridge over Bridgnorth bypass. Cross bridge then go right and at stile go left on path over 2 further stiles then across school playing fields to gap in hedge (aim 20 yards left of two sheds).
- Follow footpath down to pedestrian entrance to Bridgnorth Railway Station (home of Severn Valley Railway), cross rails carefully and go right through station car park to Railwayman's Arms.
- Take footbridge to road, go 10 yards right then cross road and up Cannon Steps.
- Go through gates opposite top of steps, past remains of Bridgnorth Castle and Thomas Telford-designed St Mary's Church, into centre of Bridgnorth.

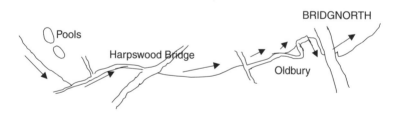

SEVERN VALLEY RAILWAY

The Severn Valley Railway was built originally in 1862 to link Hartlebury in Worcestershire with Shrewsbury, some forty miles away. This was in the great age of Railway Mania when people were putting down railway lines all over the place. Dr. Beeching saw the Severn Valley Railway off in his infamous rationalising of the railways a hundred years later but a small bunch of railways nuts in Kidderminster formed the Severn Valley Railway Society to save the line.

The restored Severn Valley Railway ran its first passenger service in May 1970, leaving Bridgnorth station at fourteen hundred hours precisely to the accompaniment of champagne corks popping. Since then, it has grown and grown in popularity and status. Its stations and its steam trains are in constant demand for period films and TV shows, while its picturesque journey through the Shropshire and Worcestershire countryside attracts thousands of visitors every weekend.

Trains on what is now commonly known as the SVR run every weekend of the year and daily at peak times between Bridgnorth and Kidderminster. There are also several special services, such as the popular Santa Specials that run over the Christmas period.

Severn Valley Railway

BRIDGNORTH PIX

Bridgnorth Castle

Market Hall

Bishop Percy's House

Richard Baxter's House

The Cartway

Cliff Railway

BRIDGNORTH STORY

"With its head up in heaven – its toes in the Severn."

Anon

Aethelfleda, daughter of King Alfred, built the first fortification in the area but it is the 1101 castle of Robert de Belleme, son of Roger of Montgomery, that claimed the dominant site in the town. The town's grid pattern was laid out in the 12th century when there were five gates guarding entrance to the town. Only one of those, Northgate, remains although what stands now is a 1910 rebuild.

The castle became the scene of the most well known event in Bridgnorth's history, when it was besieged during the Civil War. Shropshire had by and large been Royalist in its sympathies but by 1646 most of those Royalist strongholds had fallen and many of the county bigwigs moved to Bridgnorth Castle for their last defence. Parliamentary troops besieged the castle for more than three weeks. The Governor of the Castle, Sir Robert Howard, eventually surrendered when he realised that an explosion in the tunnel being built in the sandstone underneath the Castle, now known as Lavington's Hole after the engineer who built it, would kill many people. The following year the Castle was pulled down, leaving only the famous bit of its Keep, which stands at a more severe angle than the Leaning Tower of Pisa, as Bridgnorth citizens will constantly tell you.

Bridgnorth is divided by the River Severn and its two halves have become known as Low Town and High Town, which allegedly used to lead to punch-ups between the two factions. Although these still occur, they are less likely to be driven by geography. The Cliff Railway, highest inland railway in the country, joins the two parts and is well worth a ride. The alternative route is the cobbled Cartway, which bends from the river up to High Town. This was once the only connection between the two parts and was where all river goods would have been transported. In those times every house in Cartway was either a brothel or a pub. This is no longer true. The Black Boy alone remains.

The prosperity of Bridgnorth was based on its position on the River Severn. Its port in the 17th and 18th centuries being one of the busiest in Europe, as the new iron goods from Coalbrookdale were added to the existing products of carpet-weaving, leather tanning and brewing. It is now a popular commuter and tourist town, its Saturday street market and its mixture of attractive Georgian buildings and interesting pubs bringing visitors from the Black Country conurbation and further afield.

BRIDGNORTH CELEBRITIES

Richard Baxter (1615–1691)

Baxter is a key figure in the history of the Civil War. Born in poverty, he was educated by clergymen and took holy orders himself. He was appointed as the assistant minister at St Leonard's Church in Bridgnorth, where he began to be noticed for his non-conformist views. During the Civil War, he joined the Parliamentary Army, but largely to preach to the soldiers and their commanders about what he thought was right and wrong. Cromwell didn't like him but respected him and engaged in debate with him about the liberty of conscience. After the Restoration, he continued to preach his unorthodox views, which led to his eventual imprisonment when he was 70 years old by the notorious Judge Jeffreys.

Francis "Old" Moore (1657–1715)

Francis Moore was born in Bridgnorth, the son of a pauper. He taught himself to read, then set sail for London to seek his fortune, where he became a physician, a schoolteacher, and an astrologer and served at the court of Charles II. His first almanac, forecasting the weather, was published in 1699 but the biggie was *Vox Stellarum*, the Voice of the Stars, first published in 1701 and in print every year since. This became known by its present name, *Old Moore's Almanac*, and you can still buy it in Bridgnorth.

Bishop Thomas Percy (1729–1811)

Bishop Thomas Percy, whose black and white timbered house at the bottom of Cartway is one of the highlights of Bridgnorth, lived there for the first part of his life. Accidentally discovering a book of old ballads, he published them under the title *Reliques of Ancient English Poetry* in 1765, omitting the more bawdy numbers. This three-volume work was immediately successful and came to be thought of as a landmark in European literature, because it helped give birth to the Romantic Movement begun by Wordsworth and Coleridge some 40 years later.

BRIDGNORTH CAKES

CINNAMON CAFÉ, Cartway
The only fairtade café in town, serving a range of vegetarian meals and excellent home-made cakes. Very comfy seating and outside patio with good views of River Severn.

NOSTALGIA, Moat Street
Small, cosy café tucked away from view but worth visiting for high-quality cakes, teas and coffees.

CAFÉ EXPRESS, High Street
Popular meeting place in centre of town, serving freshly-made cakes, teas and coffees. Confortable seating or take a pew outside and watch the world go by.

BRIDGNORTH ALE

BEAR INN, Northgate
A former coaching inn just past the arched gate into the main street. Food at lunchtimes only. Serves several Real Ales, including Timothy Taylor Landlord. Pleasant walled beer garden out back.

BLACK BOY, Cartway
On a hill connecting the "high" and "low" towns, a pub popular with young and old for its open fire and Real Ales, Hobsons and Wood's Shropshire Lad. No food but plenty of atmosphere. Back yard has stunning views of River Severn.

KING'S HEAD, Whitburn Street
Recently refurbished to a high standard. Serves excellent Hobsons and wonderful Apley and Bishop Percy Real Ales from new Bridgnorth Brewery, plus highly-rated meals. Always busy.

RAILWAYMAN'S ARMS, Severn Valley Station
Although part of the Station, this is more than a museum, it is a live pub, with quality beer and regular beer festivals. Excellent Real Ales, including Bathams and Hobsons.

BELL AND TALBOT, Salop Street
Lovely, atmospheric little pub with two bars, serving excellent Bathams and Hobsons Real Ales plus Scrumpy cider.

BRIDGNORTH ACCOMMODATION

CROFT HOTEL, 11 St. Mary's Street, Bridgnorth, WV16 4DW
(Tel: 01746-762416)

FRIARS INN, 3 St Mary's Street, Bridgnorth, WV16 4DW
(Tel: 01746-762396 / 769521)

SEVERN ARMS HOTEL, Underhill Street, Bridgnorth, WV16 4BB
(Tel: 01746-764616)

FOX INN, 46 Hospital St, Bridgnorth, WV15 5AR (Tel: 01746-769611)

FALCON HOTEL, St Johns Street, Bridgnorth, WV15 6AG
(Tel: 01746-763134)

PARLORS HALL, Mill Street, Bridgnorth, WV15 5AL
(Tel: 01746-761931/2)

BEAR INN, 24 Northgate, Bridgnorth, WV16 4ET (Tel: 01746-763250)

BEARWOOD LODGE, Kidderminster Road, Bridgnorth, WV15 6BW
(Tel: 01746-762159)

GOLDEN LION INN, 83 High Street, Bridgnorth, WV16 4DS
(Tel: 01746-762016)

WYNDENE GUEST HOUSE, 57 Innage Lane, Bridgnorth, WV16 4HS
(Tel: 01746-764369)

SANDWARD GUEST HOUSE, 47 Cartway, Bridgnorth, WV16 4BG
(Tel: 01746-765913)

CHURCHDOWN HOUSE, 14 East Castle Street, Bridgnorth, WV16
4AL (Tel: 01746-761236)

BRIDGNORTH SERVICES

Post Office: High Street and Bridge Street

Banks with ATM: Lloyds, Barclays, Natwest, HSBC – all in High Street

Visitor Information Centre: Bridgnorth Library, Listley Street
(01746-763257)

Transport connections: Regular 890 bus service to Wolverhampton
where there is a mainline railway station.

USEFUL INFORMATION

Visitor Information Centres

Bridgnorth, Bridgnorth Library, Listley Street (01746-763257)

Cleobury Mortimer, Market Hall, High Street (Seasonal)

Ludlow, Market Square (Tel: 01584-875053)

Clun, Clun Garage, High Street (Tel: 01588-640220)

Bishop's Castle, Old Time, High Street (Tel: 01588-638467)

Church Stretton, Church Stretton Library, Church Street
(Tel: 01694-723133)

Much Wenlock, The Museum, High Street (Tel: 01952-727679)
(Seasonal)

Other Contacts

National Rail Enquiries (Tel: 08457-484950)

Shropshire Traveline (Tel: 0870-608-2608)

Shropshire Hills Area of Outstanding Natural Beauty Partnership
(Tel: 01588-674080)

Useful Websites

www.shropshirewalking.co.uk

www.shropshirehillsshuttles.co.uk

www.bridgnorthtourism.com

www.ludlow-shropshire.co.uk

www.virtual-shropshire.co.uk

SUGGESTED READING

Anon (2006), *Jack Mytton Way*, Shropshire County Council

Evans, Simon (1981), *A Simon Evans Anthology: The Poet Postman of Cleobury Mortimer*, M&M. Baldwin

Hobbs, Tony (2002), *The Pubs of Ludlow and Neighbouring Villages*, Logaston Press

Housman, A.E. (2000), *A Shropshire Lad*, Penguin Books

Hunter, David (1991), *The Shropshire Hills: a Walker's Guide*, Cicerone Press

Jones, Ian R. (1999), *The Shropshire Peaks Walk*, Ian R. Jones

Kay, Ernie & Kathy & Richards, Mark (2000), *Offa's Dyke Path South*, Aurum Press

Marsh, Terry & Meech, Julie (1999), *The Shropshire Way & Wild Edric's Way*, Cicerone Press

Marsh, Terry & Meech, Julie (1999), *Severn Way Official Walkers' Guide*, Severn Way Partnership

Marshall, John (1989), *The Severn Valley Railway*, David St John Thomas Publisher

Meech, Julie (2000), *Shropshire Towns & Villages*, Sigma Press

Palmer, Roy (2004), *The Folklore of Shropshire*, Logaston Press

Pevsner, Nikolaus (1958), *The Buildings of England: Shropshire*, Penguin Books

Protz, Roger (ed.), *Good Beer Guide 2007*, CAMRA Books

Raven, Michael (2005), *A Guide to Shropshire*, Michael Raven

Shropshire Federation of Women's Institutes (2002), *Shropshire Villages*, Countryside Books

Webb, Mary (1926), *Precious Bane*, E.P. Dutton & Co

DISTANCE CHECKLIST

SECTION ONE	DAILY MILES	TOTAL MILES
BRIDGNORTH	–	
Quatford	2	2
Chelmarsh	5	5
Billingsley	7.5	7.5
Stottesdon	10.5	10.5
CLEOBURY MORTIMER	15	15

SECTION TWO	DAILY MILES	TOTAL MILES
CLEOBURY MORTIMER	–	15
Hopton Wafers	2.5	17.5
Titterstone Clee	6	21
Cleehill	8.5	23.5
Knowbury	10.5	25.5
LUDLOW	14.5	29.5

SECTION THREE	DAILY MILES	TOTAL MILES
LUDLOW	–	29.5
Bromfield	2.5	32
Whittytree	5.5	35
Aston-on-Clun	10.5	40
Bury Ditches	15	44.5
CLUN	18	47.5

SECTION FOUR	DAILY MILES	TOTAL MILES
CLUN	–	47.5
Newcastle-on-Clun	4.5	52
Hergan	6.5	54
Churchtown	8	55.5
Reilthop	10.5	58
BISHOP'S CASTLE	14	61.5

SECTION FIVE	DAILY MILES	TOTAL MILES
BISHOP'S CASTLE	–	61.5
Linley	3	64.5
Stiperstones	6.5	68
Bridges	10	71.5
CHURCH STRETTON	15	76.5

SECTION SIX	DAILY MILES	TOTAL MILES
CHURCH STRETTON	–	76.5
Cardington	4	80.5
Wilderhope Manor	8	84.5
Wenlock Edge Inn	11	87.5
MUCH WENLOCK	15	91.5

SECTION SEVEN	DAILY MILES	TOTAL MILES
MUCH WENLOCK	–	91.5
Wyke	2.5	94
Barrow	5	96.5
Morville	10	101.5
Underton	12	103.5
BRIDGNORTH	14.5	106